ROCKSALT

ROCKSALT

An Anthology of Contemporary BC Poetry

New poetry & poetics

Edited by
Mona Fertig and Harold Rhenisch

Mother Tongue Publishing Limited
Salt Spring Island, BC
2008

LIBRARY AND ARCHIVES CANADA CATALOGUING IN PUBLICATION

Rocksalt : anthology of contemporary BC poetry / edited by Mona Fertig & Harold Rhenisch.

ISBN 978-1-896949-01-7

1. Canadian poetry (English)--British Columbia. 2. Canadian poetry (English)--21st century. I. Fertig, Mona, 1954- II. Rhenisch, Harold, 1958-

PS8295.5.B7R63 2008   C811'.60809711   C2008-903184-9

Book Design by Mark Hand

Visual Poem p. x by Judith Copithorne

Cover: oil on canvas 81.5" x 54.5" *The Poet and the Musicians,* 1996, by Diana Dean (www.dianadean.com) from The Banquet Series, courtesy of the Loch Gallery in Toronto. Private collection.

Printed and bound in Canada by Friesens

Published by:
Mother Tongue Publishing Limited
290 Fulford-Ganges Road
Salt Spring Island B.C. V8K 2K6 Canada

phone: 250-537-4155   fax: 250-537-4725
www.mothertonguepublishing.com

DEDICATION

To the poets of BC's future and to the poets who have passed, including:

Earle Birney, Michael Bullock, Fred Candelaria, Stanley Cooperman,
Gwladys V. Downes, Jon Furberg, Eric Ivan Berg, Roy Kiyooka,
Red Lane, Charles Lillard, Dorothy Livesay, Pat Lowther,
Rosalind MacPhee, Dorothy Manning, Anne Marriot, Rona Murray,
Marguerite Pinney, Roger Prentice, Helene Rosenthal, Robin Skelton,
Sharon Stevenson, Wilfred Watson and George Woodcock.

ROCKSALT POETS

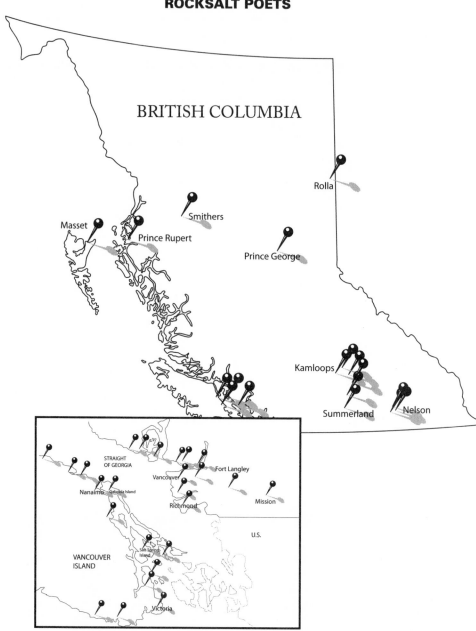

BRITISH COLUMBIA

Rolla

Smithers

Masset

Prince Rupert

Prince George

Kamloops

Summerland

Nelson

STRAIGHT
OF GEORGIA

Fort Langley

Vancouver

Nanaimo   Gabriola Island

Mission

Richmond

U.S.

VANCOUVER
ISLAND

Salt Spring
Island

Victoria

FOREWORD

Rocksalt is my first book as BC's newest literary and art trade publisher. Co-editing this long-overdue anthology has been an exciting journey. Deciding to call for new and unpublished BC poetry came from a desire to see the freshest work possible rather than present the traditional format of recycled older work. A thank-you to all the poets who sent in their poems. The decision to leave the book unthemed was energizing for many poets, although challenging for others. The freedom to write without boundaries has always been my preference. The physical act of publishing, however, provides its own limitations. Working with Harold and so many poets within a tight editing deadline certainly couldn't have been possible without email. I was very encouraged by everyone's quick response and enthusiasm. Every publisher should be so lucky. *Rocksalt* — mined from the mountains to the sea — reflects the pulse of poetry here and now: essential, sharp, salty, ancient or groundbreaking, a range of voices that sound and shift, tilt and sing within. May *Rocksalt* find its way into the schools, libraries, living rooms, and backpacks of many who live and travel here.

— Mona Fertig, *Publisher, Mother Tongue Publishing, Salt Spring Island*

INTRODUCTION

Welcome to *Rocksalt*, the first anthology of British Columbia poetry since 1977. Back then we were celebrating the publication of *New:West Coast* (Intermedia Press) and *Western Windows* (CommCept Publishing), two of the many anthologies that were recording an explosion of poetry between the Rockies and the sea. That world was transformed in the next decades, with the emergence of feminist poetry, political and work poetry, first nations' poetry, language, sound, visual and performance poetry, and poetry of the global and Asian diasporas. To all of these was added the Canadian tradition taught in our universities — perhaps best exemplified by the lyrical narrative school active in Victoria today — and the independent work of many poets across the province.

When we gathered poems for *Rocksalt*, we learned that not only had all of these poetic traditions survived, but so had many others that had never hit the literary mainstream. We discovered that British Columbians everywhere, from Neslon to Masset and Prince George to Vancouver, are writing poetry — on their kitchen tables, on scraps of paper, on old typewriters, on clunky old computers and new laptops, and are doing so as part of their daily lives. What's more, silently and miraculously, First Nations' writers had gained a voice, at the same time as much of Canadian literature had come to us. Many Canadian poets who have immigrated to BC are represented on the following pages. As many of them have been teachers, they have, in turn, raised an entire generation of young poets. These poets represent the future – one deeply enriched by an unforeseen generation of poetic engagement, reengagement, and reassessment, and with a new sense of place.

If *Rocksalt* had included all of the poets who have lived in British Columbia but for one reason or another are now living elsewhere, it would have swelled into an encyclopedia. If it had merely documented those poets living and working in BC today, it would have still run on into a manuscript of a thousand pages. We wanted a celebration, instead, and a living gift to the new generation of poets and readers. To get there, we chose to produce a snapshot of what BC poets are working on right now. As editors, we faced difficult choices. Some poets who have solidly contributed to poetry in BC for twenty or thirty years are not in *Rocksalt* because either they had no new unpublished work to send us — or because the pressures of teaching kept them from writing. Others sent us work that was so new that it was not yet ready for the press. An incredible 289 poets submitted work for *Rocksalt*. From them we selected the 108 included here. They are all represented by a new poem and a statement about their craft. They come from Bowen Island, Brentwood Bay, Burnaby, Campbell River, Cortez Island, Courtenay, Falkland, Fort Langley, Gabriola Island, Gibsons, Kamloops, Kelowna, Ladysmith, Langley, Lantzville, Madeira Park, Masset, Mission, Nanaimo, Nanoose Bay, Nelson, North Vancouver, Pender Island, Pinantan Lake, Prince George, Prince Rupert, Powell River, Qualicum Beach, Richmond, Roberts Creek, Rolla, Saanich, Salt Spring Island, Shawnigan Lake, Shirley, Sidney, Smithers, South Slocan, Summerland, Vancouver, Vernon, Victoria, West Vancouver and Winlaw.

We hope that these voices in *Rocksalt* will inspire a new generation of anthologies, like the ones that sprang up in the 1970s, which will in turn nurture a whole generation of readers. We want this to be the start of something that carries us forward for another thirty years.

– Harold Rhenisch, *Co-editor, Campbell River*

(m)utter / {st}ance, Judith Copithorne, 2005-08

CONTENTS

MALEEA **ACKER**

Maleea Acker is a writer, typographer, publisher (of La Mano Izquierda/ Left Hand Press), translator and English instructor. Her first full-length collection of poetry, *The Reflecting Pool,* will appear with Pedlar Press in 2009.

My work is informed by and centres around the natural world, and in particular, wilderness. By wilderness, I refer not only to the wild lands left to us but also to a kind of wilderness found in translation, in silence and in the threshold space that exists between one entity and another, be this person, poem, animal or landscape. I am unendingly transfixed by this threshold space, where poetry also seems most frequently found. Threshold is an idea behind my writing that first bolstered it, then stifled it (as I wondered what could possibly be an adequate response to the landscapes around me), and finally drove me to trust and seek uncertainty and thought in poetry. I no longer want definite answers in a piece. I am still searching for glimpses of the world on the other side of Tranströmer's "wall" but I now appreciate, more and more, the draw of an unmasked poem, one that thinks, hesitates, questions and is willing to come face to face with the other. More and more for me, this encounter contains not only astonishment and awe, but also humour and joy. To sustain my work, I walk, I fall in love with small hills in the Pyrenees, and I try to attend to small pieces of southern Vancouver Island ecosystems, in words or by action.

Tree Frogs

It's singing outside.
   Beginning in
awkward twosome, the
syncopation all
     wrong, then they get it together and rise
and fall from perfect to trios
to perfect to
green popcorn,
  berry husks
     or rye grass jumping open at touch.

 I'm as thin as the skin
that connects my dog's belly with her thigh.
She's dreaming beside me.
    In her mind green stretches for miles,
the lily pad corridor opens into light
ironed smooth and live.
   She trails the boat.
     She's a hollow reed that smiles.

  When I was nine
I counted minutes with friends until my birth time.
4:08 pm. The embroidered chair, the skylight
of my mother's room, the step
 I fell from and lost
a tooth on, the drop into something deep—
   pining, not to be followed by this sadness, having lost
the single number, casting up
     for the thing gone.
Then a silence.
A little more than twenty years.

  In Catalunya
Lleone hill grows green since I've gone.
   The bells move to summer pasture and the stream's twisting, twisting,
    it pulls away
from everything, frogs in its head rush,

can't be touched without affection,
    doesn't glitter under birch and grasses and cliffs but takes
their colour and bends it
      until blue
   snaps free from green: swallows,
        sea wind, blue so blue it's shaking in its sleep.

JOANNE **ARNOTT**

Joanne Arnott is a Metis/mixed blood writer from Winnipeg. She studied English briefly at the University of Windsor then moved to the West Coast in 1982. Joanne has presented workshops and performed her work across much of Canada and in Australia. She worked for many years as an Unlearning Racism facilitator, and continues to incorporate social justice perspectives in her work. Her first book, *Wiles of Girlhood* (Press Gang) won The League of Canadian Poets' Gerald Lampert Award. Five books followed, most recently *Steepy Mountain: love poetry* (Kegedonce Press) and *Mother Time: Poems New & Selected* (Ronsdale Press). Joanne is mother to five sons and one daughter, all born at home; she lives with her family in Richmond, BC.

When I arrived in Vancouver after my brief stay at university, I became steeped in the landscape and healed by it as well: this was a thoroughly urban experience, featuring transit buses and hours & hours & hours on my own two feet, looking, walking. I saw that the tree at the roadside, the ocean at my feet, the mountains curling high over my right shoulder, I myself, and all of humanity besides, were works in progress: we were waves, each wave affecting the others, each wave unfolding in its own rhythmic scale of space and time. Through my immersion in the living culture of Vancouver, through its libraries and the small Taoist tan I attended, the kung fu and tai chi classes, I found words for all of this raw data I was gathering, in Chinese traditional science and Taoist religion. Through my participation in co-operative enterprises, I learned about structural applications of democracy. Later, becoming immersed in the healing work being done by and among urban Indians, through traditional and adapted First Nations ceremonial approaches, my sense of home, heart and community were deepened, lengthened and restored. In real world spiritual practise, I follow prairie teachings. In poetry, the grandmothers & grandfathers visit, and the image of the goddess is my most frequent expression of divinity.

As a writer, I express the wave of my own unfurling. If I want to know what is going on, I write a poem. I write an essay. I write all along the edges of myself, on the interface between the known and the unknown, and I listen to the words like a seer listens to dreams. My poetry is not fiction. I am a creator, and I both grapple with and invent the world through the writing of my poems.

she is riding

down through the suburban grey
streets dreamed by developers and
implemented for traffic floes

comes riding the turquoise green grandmother
riding her mighty Sow
onto the battlefield

down along the highway of decay she rides
between the crack houses and on to piggy palace
where the spirits of the women are lifted

out of the horror, out of the muck, like
troubled teeth and bone fragments
their spirits gather and rise, and rise

all of our dead sisters lifted by those winged women
well-versed in the protocols of the battlefields
recognizing the existence of the battlefields, here

as along the highway of tears

shoulders back
open arms
open chested

the turquoise green grandmother breathes
along with each one of us still travelling
our inner city streets

our turns on the quiet highways
our love affairs gone wrong
our villages overrun

shoulders back
open arms
open chested

letting flow the sounds of the inside
the sounds of our voices calling out songs of sorrow
the sounds of our drums rising through time and through sky
the sounds of our warm bodies travelling swift
through the families
and through the forests

shoulders back
open arms
open chested

we accompany our sisters and brothers to the threshold
we hold them until they are fled, and then
we hold them more

we accompany our mothers and our fathers
we accompany our children, our friends, and o
the many strangers, the star gazers

we hold our dying persons long
dwell inside memory

we lay each one to rest
slowly

shoulders back
open arms
open chested

tears coursing from the inside
across the outside and wetting
our multihued skins

the touch of a warm palm in passing
through hair on a child's head gently

the touch of a lover to beloved
any where, at any time

the touch of a grandmother's warm palm
on the cheek of her adult offspring

or along the stiff hair on the Sow's back
she is riding

JOHN **BARTON**

John Barton has published eight books of poetry and five chapbooks, including *Sweet Ellipsis* (1998), and *Hypothesis* (2001). A bilingual edition of his third book, *West of Darkness: Emily Carr, a self-portrait*, was published in 2006; his ninth collection, *Hymn*, is forthcoming from Brick in 2009. Co-editor of *Seminal: The Anthology of Canada's Gay Male Poets* (2007), he has won three Archibald Lampman Awards, a Patricia Hackett Prize, an Ottawa Book Award, a 2003 CBC Literary Award and a 2006 National Magazine Award. The former editor of Ottawa's *Arc*, he lives in Victoria, where he edits *The Malahat Review*. In 2008–2009, he is writer in residence at Saskatoon Public Library.

My creative interests revolve around three keys: the body, visual art and the built and natural environments. I bring to these a sensibility that sees language as a diagnostic. I consider the written text to be the median between the reader and the writer; each brings his or her own experience to it and changes it subtly. Therefore, while fixed in language, the poem itself is unstable and mutable, open to multiplying and perhaps contradictory interpretations. It is also a time capsule that carries forward signs of what it is (and was) like to be alive in one place and time. Because I foreground gay sensibility in my work, I also see words as charged politically, necessary tools of enlightenment and disruption. We read (and write) for two reasons: to see ourselves and to dialogue with the unknown. Art is about pleasure and engagement; validation and interrogation.

Jon Extracting a Splinter

Paul Cadmus (1904–1999)
NM 255, crayon on paper, 1993

The observed absorbed, forgetting your regard—his

Body on paper, drawn sitting on the floor.
To the uninvolved, unconsciously
Posed. Naked as usual.

Knees raised and apart, bent slightly as he leans forward over
The task, intimate and known, feet at rest
On their sides, heel
Of the left about to nest in the unseen
Arch of the right, but for what the fingers
Of one hand loosen.
                            Or perhaps the legs would stretch out
More fully and the ankles
Cross, the eyes lift to
Meet the eyes
Of his beloved—your eyes—briefly, but for the pose, but
For what his fingers loosen.

What the fingers loosen.
The crosshatching.
The concentration.

The arms long and powerful come to rest on the calves
Almost in parallel, leading the eye.
The eye straying, completing the body

Touching on the crown, long wavy blonde hair
Whitening and pulled back, moving
Along the neck and shoulder, hunched over the haunches, lingering
Over the trapezoids of obliques and rib cage towards
The curve of the buttock, ubiquitous

Penis uncircumcised, but
Never circumspect, however hooded
And discretely glimpsed from under his crooked right knee.

The mind bent to the task.
The body rising from the impartial dark.

Risen from beige uncoated paper, held
Down by the patient
Laid lines
Of pastel—brown, yellow, pink—each one distinct

But from a distance a blur of soft

Aging constancies of skin, white imposed
To connote
Light and its inclination

To fall—across the body, in line, seemingly, with the history
Of art, however often withheld the vulnerable
Lineage of the male—the impaled

Toe almost in shadow, to you at least—
Perhaps not to the beloved.

BILL **BISSETT**

arrivd on erth from lunaria ovr 300 yeers ago in lunarian time as part uv th first childrns shuttul 2 erth wch landid in halifax nova scotia workd blewointment press 4 sum 20 erthling yeers love sound poetree vizual poetree politikul non narrativ n othr forms paint as well most recent book *ths is erth thees ar peopul* from talonbooks 07 most recent cds *deth interrupts th dansing* with composr pete dako from red deer press 06 *n ths is erth thees ar peopul* with pete dako from blu loon prod 08 up cumming book *sublingual* fall 08 talonbooks hope 2 keep on xlooring all th wayze uv breething with words

bcoz i have gemini rising   partlee bcoz ium eklektik n appresiate th depth uv varietee i write in abt sevn wayze approaches 2 poetree ths is not bettr not wors thn a poet who writes in wun or mor approaches   its onlee what i dew is thees lyrikul loves lost n found n continuing what goez in2 th sereen moment sound vizual narrativ politikul working 4 mor egalitarian models 4 us all 2 live with toppuling th klass hierarkeez uv anee kind langwage gives us th tools 4 soshul change   his her storikul non narrativ all thees shapings can fold in n out uv each othr fueseyun poetree in wch thees elements all can b in th wun kontainr pomes uv protest against unjust wars   meditativ metaphysikul spiritual   opn mouth opn heart realism konversaysyunal vois   voices talking 4 th environment th beautee uv naytur how we need it 2 thrive 2 b if we destroy naytur we kill ourselvs th realizaysyun uv dreems etching in th luminous tray uv longings desires feers holdings th words ar all parts uv speech yernings let ting them thru disturbing murmurs symbols kolours sounds uv th erth our mytholojeez uv permanens cries skreems in th nite embeddid in th human condishyuns feetyurs uv such boiling trubuls n positiv elixirs neurologikal endorpheena   poetree wun uv th most ancient uv arts still n fleeting th moments uv serenitee brillyant vibrant etchd in our beings

going thru th arktik

i didint think ther wud b no mor trew love songs   wher wud they happn whn
th sky is mango green

i didint think ther wud b no mor trew love
songs   whn g-d th great spirit takes us
back in2 goldn sleep 2 sew n harvest agen

trew love songs ar a dreem as we push
thru ths desert uv ice   yes 2 sorrow n yes 2 blessing songs

i thot i wud b sew glad 2 cum home i am sew glad 2 cum home

wher wer yu in th estrangd hotel i lookd
4 yu in th seedee restaurant   i devourd
previous tropes lost jestyurs th old barbr shop

th cameos uv sum wuns ancestors th
swimming pools uv th eyez uv th ancient wuns theyr hands ar reeching out
from th elektrik plasma b brave deep breething keep on looking childrn we
found each othr agen no romans 2 mess things up hey we can
play agen th snakes at last kavorting ovr th stinkee furnitur

ths is wher th song cums in in th middul
uv evreething in a hiddn away sacrid n calm place in a street car going 2 work
trew love or not th deer in th 4est
dust in th mining town th faces looking out ovr th mountain from th abandond
hotel windos

  n wud th song cum agen
   n yes th song is cum agen

      eye embrace yu within th narrow
   transparent walls uv our dreems
   th sumtimes ar setting uv our brokn
       hearts n we can hang now hang now hanging now   hanging now

       n th ocean voyage

kontinuez hey look
at th whales look at th
whales yes

YVONNE **BLOMER**

Yvonne Blomer's poetry has won awards and been published internationally in such journals as *Seam, the Rialto, Grain* and *The Malahat Review* in addition to being in *In Fine Form: An Anthology of Canadian Form Poetry*. She gained an MA in Poetry, Distinction from The University of East Anglia in 2006. Her first book, *a broken mirror, fallen leaf* was short listed for The Gerald Lampert Memorial Award in 2007.

One of my main interests in writing the poems in *The Birds of the Bible*, from which The Camel and the Bird was taken, is to question the self-centeredness of humanity in view of the world. My hope is to explore the assumptions, stereotypes and roles of animals, birds specifically, in the biblical stories and beliefs. I also want to explore the wildness of the birds and the taming that occurs when writing about them. The poems are subjective; they aim to place the human world and the natural world in a face-to-face interaction in the hopes that the reader will step back and begin to see in a new way.

The Camel and the Bird

Patere

And he made his camels to kneel down without the city by a well of water
at the time of the evening, even the time that women go out to draw water.
                    Genesis 24:11

Camel, cousin to grace,
the humped, the never thirsty,
you have the appearance of one
sated, so sage in your tenacity.
At the well, always there is a well,
and some wandering soul in need,
and you, forty days and as many
nights your tongue has sat
heavy as muddied leather. Docile
your moulded shape, sculpted to the walls
of your patron, in the church of St. Francis,
in a village where time has stood
testament to you. *Patere.*
Oh how you do, you do endure.

Abstine

and that the humble friars, like little birds, should possess nothing in this world,
but should cast all the care of their lives on the providence of God.
          From Little Flowers of St. Francis of Assisi

On the rock mound, go to the rocks,
and on the dry bed of earth, taste it;
seeds left to feed you,
Chukar, taste your name,
let it melt, name yourself –
Chogka, Hag'l, Rock
Partridge, *Alectoris grace* –
cannibal that flesh, hear it.
Savour, as you do, you do,
savour the dry mouth, the hunger.
In the coloured bands, in the red-rimmed
eyes, the red feet, see yourself.
In the fledglings, now fleeing.
In the egg, and the cock,
in the brightness and beauty of melanin,
your black bright stripes, know it.
Here is beauty, and here you abstain from it;
food piled around, little dark flush.
You will leave it, and you will leave it
etched to the wall in the church of St. Francis.
You will pluck up your wings,
you will rest, rest in the hand of that man,
and he will blow breath into you
and you will flee it.

ALLISON **BLYTHE**

Allison Blythe was born in 1976 in Coburg, Ontario. On September 1, 1985, she moved to Victoria, British Columbia, with her sister and mother. That day she also crashed her new Free Spirit bicycle into a massive UVic blackberry bush and was pulled out by a thoughtful secretary. She was bloodied but home. Allison now lives with her partner on the Gorge Waterway. Her poetry hopes to explore the places of contact between natural and artistic worlds.

My process is very much like a songbird taking a bath: dipping under and slicking feathers close, then ruffling them back out in the air, over and over. The hope, in poetry, is that at some point a balance is reached where what is left out of the poem and what is left in are singing to each other. I believe each poem has its own needs for line length, rhyme, structure and rhythm; I believe more deeply that every poem flashes into being from the same place of attention — a place with a distinct and consistent resonance. The best poetry, for me, balances spontaneity with careful attention.

Greet the Light

In the first seconds of life
light is pulled over our heads
like a plain work shirt.

It's later we learn of Vermeer and God
shaking light like white fire ants in their fists,
flinging the winged bodies over

the wet stem of a ship, gather
of a woman's skirt, pearl
glow of an open window. And even beyond

this ecstatic labour, Earth
subducts, knuckles over, forces fire
from a necklace of volcanoes.
                                        No one said:

go on, get to it. There was no more room
in darkness. Still though,
after that first elemental rush,

how irreparable the light.

LEANNE **BOSCHMAN**

Leanne Boschman has lived over half her life in British Columbia — mostly in the Northwest. At the present time she has two homes — Shawnigan Lake and Prince Rupert. As a prairie transplant, she has come to appreciate the lushness, the largeness of the landscape. Her prairie self does sometimes find the dark winters too intense, and she gets a little melancholy. Good for writing poetry, she hopes. She finds herself on the verge of having an empty nest, wondering if perhaps she'll have more time for writing. Perhaps. She also teaches English at Northwest Community College.

In the Mennonite tradition I grew up in, music and oratory (as in sermons) were deeply valued. So although I am aware that poetry has a musical heritage and pay attention to metre, rhyme and sound texture in the crafting of my poems, I also explore the relationship between text and orality through spoken word practices. Some of these practices include memorization, blocking and singing during the performance of poetry, and I believe these practices help me to reach a broader audience. Recently, I have been exploring the sacred song/chant movement and am intrigued by the rich and complex relationship between orality and literacy in the realm of devotional scripture, poetry and song. Participants in chant circles sing sacred verses in Sanskrit, Arabic, Latin, First Nations languages, etc. They practice "toning" to experience purely vibrational/energetic connections. It strikes me that these connections are what bp Nichol was referring to in his chant/poem "Pom Poem."

As far as subject matter goes, I resist the pressure to write about "happy" subjects underlying the comment often directed at poets, "Why are so many poems about the dark side of experience"? What I appreciate in poems and strive for in my own is that sense of experience pared down to its essential details, where what is both lost and gained in a single moment becomes apparent. Both joy and sorrow revolve around this realization. Well, that's something to aim for, anyway.

Wintersong

for Butch Dick, Songhees Nation

At a sacredsong festival when I could have been whirling
ecstatically or chanting ancient Hebrew invocations,
I sat instead in the sanctuary, shivered with the others
in a small circle. Fogged windows behind dark brown
beams of the cross, winter had been rugged, was getting old.
In a quiet voice you told us that some songs can be shared
while others belong to families, clans, and ceremonies.
But there are small everyday songs, like ones you heard
your mother and grandmother sing while working,
those mending basket songs we keep nearby, or tucked
into pockets for long afternoons when we might need them —
songs that keep our spirits strong.

You told us about the drums, how newcomers must
observe the mouth of the singer, then softly enter the song,
how it is important to sing only as big as the place you're in;
that's why singing is different on the plains and in the forest.
Some kids join the group, you said, only for the cupcakes;
they soon leave but others stay.
Lines of muffled notes wrapped like moss around branches
soaked dark with rain, a tangled song was creaking in my chest.

Your grandmother spoke no English and you no Lekwungen —
summers when she told you to get wood you brought water,
when she told you to fetch water you brought wood,
but as weeks went by, you understood more, loved more.
I thought of summers with my own grandparents, hearing
the language that my parents spoke only when they didn't
want *die Kinder* to understand, but we did and could tell
they spoke their Plaudietsch poorly.
In a sweet baritone, Grandfather sang hymns before meals.
Once when my brothers and I imprisoned butterflies in jars,
he said *frie an*—free them, and we did.

At the edge of a small Saskatchewan town I walked beside
him on unbroken prairie, pulled up tufts of sage to sniff,
filled my pockets with stones. We came upon a teepee ring,
weathered stones encrusted with lichen, once the base
of a home, inhabitants gone now, but I knew this circle
of stones belonged to that ground, belonged to earth.
In the Zoar Mennonite Church his funeral was observed
with black clothing and restrained tears, but a ten year old's
sobs rose above a solemn hymn and hard wooden benches.
My mother did not hush me or frown disapproval,
she took her watch off, not the everyday one, but a delicate
gold expansion bracelet and slipped it over my thin wrist.
She smiled at me, held my hand. Time moved in a circle—
here I was again in a church, thinking of my grandfather,
how it had been thirty-eight years since I had heard
his voice, a soft but stern voice like yours.
I thought about the two grandsons you were raising,
how you must sing to them, teach them to play drums,
hum the Lehal Victory Song.

A circle song to close—I carefully watched your mouth
as you described how suddenly a singer feels a fastening,
a connecting of the circle in that song from flatlands,
wordless song that gathered our secrets like small pebbles,
song strong enough to encompass our sorrows,
all of us singing our histories, singing our way home
in song our voices joined,   ooh, oh, oh
load of silence lifted all in song,   hey, hey

MARILYN **BOWERING**

Marilyn Bowering has received many awards for poetry including the Pat Lowther Award, the Dorothy Livesay Prize and several National Magazine awards. Her work has twice been nominated for the Governor General's Prize. Recognition for Marilyn Bowering's fiction includes the Ethel Wilson Prize, designation of Notable Book by the New York Times, and short-listing for the world-wide Orange Prize. Her most recent books are *Green* (poetry) and *What It Takes To Be Human* (novel). Marilyn Bowering has travelled extensively: she now lives with her family in Sooke, BC.

I grew up during the Cold War. The 20th century, like every century before, was littered with war, famine, tyrants, genocide — and these things continue into the 21st century. At some level, though, human beings (and perhaps particularly the descendants of immigrants) believe at a profound level that there is hope for a positive evolution, for a better future. In a country like Canada, the evidence of this confronts us daily, especially in the natural world. I live at the edge of a forest and near the sea. At night I can watch the stars and feel connected with every other person who has lived and looked at the sky. Poetry is able to convey these parallel worlds of chaotic human experience and intrinsic beauty and order. It takes us out of the chaos, lets us stand back and understand even while we are deeply involved in the process of living terrible contradictions. To me, a poem is like this — it eddies in the stream of human experience. It's as if the poem is a cup dipped into this water and lifted so that, through its often astonishing forms and imagery, we can see clearly the one thing we need to see, or find ourselves able to conceive of what we'd thought was inconceivable. This is very grand, and not every poem or maybe any of mine, achieves it. What matters more is that the poet with her tools of inherited language (honed by centuries of life and usage) and music (the oral roots that define what a poem can be) senses there are different ways of knowing and tries to make the poem a bridge for herself and others. Nothing is explained, but it is given another dimension through the words, sound and energy of the poet, that may be, itself, a kind of love or grace.

Colour Theory

Let us say (so much saying to do!)
that the blue of heaven is brought forth

from the imagination of god
or an equivalent of god, which could be

the sum total of the force that spins
from a cast away body

that perceives not only the green forest
perimeter of the world

but paint and wooden walls
and the comfort of couch and chair
and carpet:

this harmony

is conjured like taste
by the practice of centuries. Some

hope themselves a net,
and some use their hands,

and what's caught there's
a chemical
reaction— the base metal

of a body that burns to gold: just

for a second the black sky
is seared with stars and the writing is plain.

It's a theory, I guess, that any good will come,
but I have my hand in my mothers hair,

and my father is in my arms,
and against my breast—

such children as could make you believe.

KATE **BRAID**

Kate Braid has published four prize-winning books of poetry, most recently, *A Well-Mannered Storm: The Glenn Gould Poems*. She also co-edited with Sandy Shreve the first Canadian book of formal poetry, *In Fine Form*. In addition to numerous essays, she has published three books of creative non-fiction and is currently writing her memoir of fifteen years as a carpenter. She lives with her partner in Burnaby, BC.

In my naïve and foolish adolescence and young adulthood, I was often misled by intellect; I was easily dazzled by language and for a long time figured that to be incomprehensible was to be wise. Then I became a feminist. I got older. I had a few hard falls and now I am more cautious. Now I have a compass that is my body, instinct that speaks clearly – and listens – from my gut. Now I find that for words to be merely pretty or merely clever is not enough. The reason we talk to each other – all those exchanges that make up culture and community – is connection. And if I – a careful reader – do not understand your words then you, the careful writer, must help me make the connection so I can see the wonder there. Then what I already know becomes a compass, a ground, now pointing at what I don't know, would like to know, never even realized I need to know. This is a test I apply to my own writing as well as to what I read. I'm no longer any good at blind faith, at taking other people's word for it. Now I think both of us – reader and writer – must work harder than that. And the line thrown between us, the connection, will be some form of narrative – sometimes a thread and sometimes a hawser – of shared meaning. Now we're talking.

I Used to Drink

not gaily,
but with
a whiskey hammer every night
that drowned
the dullness of a day spent
denying
the things that were woman of me.

Small thing, the men said.
The taste was bitter

but easier
than pulling out individual pinpricks
of pain.

> *I wouldn't let my wife do this.*
> *Want to see a dirty movie after work?*

Once I drank
all night, so
in the morning, gold
everything looked – didn't it? –
bright.

Red wine, brandy, scotch or gin,
it didn't matter. All poultices.

Desperate not to drink alone, I'd
beg, jibe, challenge, jeer,
anything
to make you keep me
a wet, a weary company.
Don't leave me, I said,

terror like an awkward duck
rising roughly off its pond.
I swallowed harder.

A double.

So many terrors:
the terror I might not be able to do this,
the terror that maybe they were right
(*only a woman* and all that).

I drank as if I were a flower, dried up
and seeking rain.
I drank as if it would open a closed vein
of wonder.
I drank as prayer, as petition,
as penance, as plea.

I like you now, the other carpenters said.
I like you soft, a little unfocussed,
A little loaded, not all that
unladylike push and buzz.

Drunk, I acknowledged anger.
Went home.
Dead sober.

BRENDA **BROOKS**

Brenda Brooks has written two poetry collections, *Somebody Should Kiss You* and *Blue Light in the Dash*, and a novel, *Gotta Find Me an Angel*, shortlisted for the Books in Canada/Amazon.ca First Novel Award in 2005. She has been included in anthologies in Canada, the U.S and Great Britain. She is currently working on a collection of poetry.

I can think of no better words concerning poetry than the following small excerpt from Pablo Neruda's wonderful essay *Toward An Impure Poetry*, where he speaks of the themes he believes make up the lifeblood of poetry: poetry impure as the clothing we wear, or our bodies, soup-stained, soiled with our shameful behaviour, our wrinkles and vigils and dreams, observations and prophecies, declarations of loathing and love, idylls and beasts, the shocks of encounter, political loyalties, denials and doubts, affirmations and taxes.

Betrayal

Waking, I remember my hands.
Oh not these beat-up buddies moaning
in each others' arms at midnight.
Not this forlorn twosome crouched
behind the window while winter steals
the neighbour's doghouse one pretty
second at a time. I mean my real hands,
before desertion of all dazzle and cha
cha cha. My real hands deft and wild,
who never had a thing for that pair
of broke-down mongrels out there
in the blizzard curled up in their sad, sinking abode;
not a cookie or scrap of scratch-behind-the-ears solace
for their heartbroken dreams of the dark, distant
forest of their beginnings; far beyond the last hydro cut,
when the moon was their brother and they slipped
through the forest with night in their teeth.

HOWARD **BROWN**

Howard Brown is a writer and visual artist living in the north Okanagan. He has a BA(Hon) and MA in Philosophy and over the years has been a roughneck, sailor, coal miner, teacher and has spent the last 25 years as an industrial electrician. He has self-published two poetry collections and a chapbook and has had his work published in *Quills Canadian Poetry, Ascent Aspirations, Trade Talk Magazine, Pinebeetle Press* and *CPA Anthology: Harvesting Treasures*. He is a studio artist at Gallery Vertigo in Vernon, BC and a director on the board of the Shuswap Association of Writers in Salmon Arm, BC.

I love the economy of poetry. In almost every case each re-write is shorter and more succinct than the previous version. Yet as a poet I keep running into the limits of language desperately wanting to speak the ineffable. There is no word. The metaphor doesn't quite do the job. Something wants saying that can't quite be said. On the other hand everything is fair game as subject matter: a memory, a proposition from a prostitute, the smell of a KFC outlet on a hot day. For me writing poetry is liberating — an outlet for political and social commentary, an opportunity for whimsical word play or to engage in satire. It is a way to lay bare some feeling or convey some picture and it is a way to tell a story without a lot of words.

When the World Was Not So Scared

two rooms and a cook stove
cheap linoleum worn to the black
cracks of daylight where the stovepipe pokes the roof
the old woman bakes bread in jam cans
her loaf tins had burned with the house in harder times
a clock ticks holes in the silences
between her age and ours
wearing a dark bonnet
her profile is that of a witch from our fairy-tale book
she will not cook and eat us though
but give us fresh bread from her jam cans
we are fascinated by the round slices
we call her grandma though she isn't ours
she hollers out the door for her son
to come for bread and tea
he's middle aged and bald but she calls him boy
his cabin is across the yard
one room with a bearskin on the bed
it smells unwashed mixed with Ogdens Fine Cut tobacco
he teaches me to play cribbage there
my brother and I are not afraid to follow the ruts
that lead us here through the bush
though we are small children
our mother and father do not worry
the world was not so scared then

TREVOR **CAROLAN**

Trevor Carolan has published two collections of poetry – *Closing The Circle* (Heron Press) and *Celtic Highway* (Ekstasis). His essays and interviews are read internationally, and he has produced books of fiction, memoir, translation and anthologies. He was literary co-ordinator for the XV Olympic Winter Games in Calgary, and has been Director of writing and publishing programs at the Banff Arts Centre. A veteran community activist, he served as elected municipal councillor in North Vancouver and has been a political columnist. He earned an interdisciplinary Ph.D. in International Relations and teaches English at the University of the Fraser Valley.

I try to keep it simple. Thanks to my high-school creative writing teacher, Sam Roddan, in New Westminster, my poetry aired on CBC before it was ever published. This taught me early on the responsibility of having an audience. Music and theatre called me elsewhere, but I returned to poetry in the late 1970s. My sense of what a living poetry could be was shaped through attending readings at The Literary Storefront in Vancouver's Gastown. Through hearing and reading many excellent local writers I saw that it was possible to simply write from the West Coast, to be a good hometown poet, to write from the heart about this place. With an interest in the Beats, I've always enjoyed poetry with a strong sense of engagement, so advocacy and even investigative poetics are part of my artistic grounding. As a longtime practitioner of Tai Chi, I've observed how it brings a certain nature awareness into my work, and this is also an essential element in the whole Pacific Northwest literary tradition that is important for many of us in BC. The regard for meditative stillness that arises in my poems derives pretty clearly from my ongoing Buddhist practice. Having raised a family, I see too how often my work celebrates small epiphany moments — berry picking, summer campfire evenings, fishing with the kids and our elders, sighting a memorable landform or shoreline together. I love collaborating as poet-librettist with musicians and others: it's a fruitful way of pulling many of my personal interest areas together. Probably it's an old Auden and Spender impulse, but through my teaching in recent years I'm noticing a sharper appetite for the demands of classical metrical forms.

My Old Master Eats Cherries

Toothless, shriven-cheeked,
munching on their sweetness...
He's confined to wheelchair now,
afghan on lap,
ninety-seven and bruised from I.V. drips and needles.

His old skin flakes,
urine odour in air;
wrapped in sports togs, off-balance in his chair;
five years ago, he still sparred with the best of us,
three, four at a time.

We talk, but he forgets. We laugh.
He munches the cherries,
expensive, but what's money for?
Maybe a shave would help him, his
hair still monkish short. Old—old.

At ninety-seven, he's gotten cranky as hell,
ancient in fact;
wears glasses with a name-tag.
We work at laughter,
slapstick stories, me as the nutty straight-man.

My heart breaks at the sight of him.
He taught me most everything I know.

KEN **CATHERS**

Ken Cathers has been published in numerous periodicals and anthologies over the years, most recently *Island Writer* and *Prism International*. He has also recently published (spring 2008) his fifth book of poetry, *Blues For The Grauballeman* (Ekstasis Press).

I have tried to write poetry that evokes a sense of place, that involves narrative as a means to the immediate and immanent. I have tried to create a music out of my personal idiom and the crude beauty of the coast.

sons

my father left
no words
    to relieve this
    emptiness.

a quiet man
from a silent
    country

he left no stories
to grow on
no dreams
    to believe.

my sons
I come from
    a dark settlement

know only the music
of cries
    & whispers:

        a sad inheritance.

my sons
    I have spent
    my whole life
        rebuilding

constructing a shelter
of words
    against the storm
    I cannot escape

part of everything
you have
so easily
    left behind.

KAREN **CHESTER**

Karen Chester is a freelance writer, editor, poet and sometimes ethnographic consultant. Friday night poetry at The Black Stilt Coffeehouse is a highlight of her week, along with the antics of her two children.

After is a remembrance of my grandmother who encouraged us to swim, no matter what the weather, or our age, in the buff at Ardmore, near Victoria. And if we had a scrape, she insisted that we bathe in seawater. Betty Gillespie died on August 20th, 2007, but was able to listen to this poem before her passing.

After

Rising early, I do not bathe
but linger on the patio
terrycloth gown wrapped close
holds me to the night

ribbons of steam, coffee on the table
a dreamer's milky way
lifting fingers, one at a time
to smell you again

the noon sun has crept its way up the sky
I shower
not without regret
let water rivulet down my cheek
hair, seaweed tangles about my shoulders

examining the ragged edges of a barnacle cut
my grandmother would say, *salt water heals*
and she'd send me back in
waves lap about my ankles,
a sudden splash up the inside of my thighs
takes me by surprise, deeper than I'd intended.

JUDITH **COPITHORNE**

Recently have had work in the publications *fhole, industrial sabotage, West Coast Line, Rain Review of Books*, and *curvd H&Z* and online at *W & The News*. Born in Vancouver in 1939, I remember voices wavering amongst the whistling and rushing shortwave radio sounds which I imagined were the sounds of the ocean. I remember the smelts running so thickly at Spanish Banks that you could catch them in your towel. And I remember the fleet of fish boats sailing, each summer night, into English Bay, in a single row, their lights gradually coming on as night fell. This took over an hour and was one of the most beautiful processions I have ever seen.

Poetry needs synthesis. The world contains hundreds of languages and literatures which more and more often form and reform each other. In the 1960s, personal expression was important. Now the personal is less important, and abstraction has increased. Young people continue to have new ideas. The body of feminist literature continues to expand, as does radical and egalitarian work in many forms. If grammar is innate, then language is also and so, probably, is poetry; thus, whatever our methods of writing, if we don't take this instinctive basis into account, our writing will dry up. Poetry predates particular traditions and schools and will continue beyond our innovations, for poetry is bigger than each of us. — And yet we want to grow beyond our instinctual roots: as we hope to become less violent and selfish, so our minds help us to see how our will and our intentions might express themselves. Theory contains intellectual speculation, which is an interesting form of connection to poetry. So, although theoretical poetry may not produce the affects of other types of poetry, it can stimulate intellectual passion. Pure humor opens the mind, satire and irony sharpen it, sonic qualities and imagery sway it. Sound and visual poetries add further dimensions. Today modernist, lyrical, language-oriented and surreal poetry are only a few of the forms available to us. It is fascinating to sample the great riches available across the spectrum of poetry. Why not experiment with this wide range of poetry and experience its gifts of the mind, of the emotions and of the senses?

Heliocentricity

In the beginning was the sun and in Helios we lived as
electromagnetic energy bursting from sunspots of one hundred
million degrees of heat, of light. Bursting into life, while roseation
hammers absolute deficits, spherically enhanced, needed
compassion, economic democracy, requitement and solved autocracy
of greed.

Let us accept the extreme importance of our appearance here today to
hear how colloidal solutions are the gold of the alchemy of trust, of
the electricity of honour, of the rationality of truth and the specific
density of a general strike. Oh sorority of the belief in the body in the
coffin of bad governance.

narrow rows some flown eons rise ions soar ones below sonar
sighs

Then finally we salute and behave sweetly, up and out of silky
endorphins's slick release, wishing satiated desire, gentle intimacy.

Salutary deceiving, despair roiling, uncouth, duplicitous, collusion
in this lovely array rising through our ionosphere in oxytoxish
satisfaction, all this time screaming, "Out of my mind over you, my
lost lust, my ancient coeval twin."

Scores of contaminants course through our veins, hearts & minds & yet
we are alive now in the dawn of lilies, this time of our poor, foolish
hopes, corrupted & endlessly redeemed by worms and dark and light
matter. Fight, flight, desolate tectonic plates buckle & shiver, electrons
flip, move out of orbit. Green hazes over the music of our
understanding.

muons dendrites elliptical apogees rocked in shale chromium silica
germanium carbon periodic elemental rhythms

Now, kind, puzzled comrades, bound in the matter & the energy of
our design, our nexus of need, our unlovely glamour. The venerable
ocean draws back around us, the gale bucks over waves, gulls scream,

salt envelopes and breakers enfold us and we are part of sea, sky and the distant possibility of solutions.

SUSAN **CORMIER**

Metis multimedia writer Susan Cormier has won or been shortlisted for such awards as CBC's National Literary Award, Arc Magazine's Poem of the Year, and the Federation of BC Writers' Literary Writes. Her writing has appeared in publications including *Blood and Aphorisms New Fiction, Atlantis: A Women's Studies Journal, West Coast Line, Arc,* and two provincial anthologies. Susan has been artist-in-attendance at the herland feminist film festival, a founding editor of *Rain City Review* magazine, and a Western Canada representative on the SlamAmerica national performance poetry tour. Current projects include "Three on the Tree," a screenplay examining memory and identity.

Music and poetry are a manifestation of the oral tradition which has played a vital role in the documentation and preservation of cultures, ideas, and religions throughout history. As word artists, our role is that of "storykeepers": we document and share stories which are important to present and future understanding of the culture and society we are part of.

I began studying music at the age of three and was writing songs by my early teens. Following a car accident in my mid-teens, I lost the ability to read and play music, but continued to write songs. Faced with the inability to translate the music in my head into a tangible form, I turned to poetry, and eventually to performance, video and sculpture. Recently, I have returned to my roots through the use of musical elements such as singing, rhyme and song-like structure.

North American Indigenous cultures have similarly experienced a loss of language and culture through trauma and outside interference. Present generations, however, are returning to their culture's roots of communication. Music, dance, spoken word and craft are increasing in popularity as artists of Indigenous backgrounds overcome the challenge of the loss of tongue and tradition to reclaim ancient forms of communication and create new forms of music, art and storytelling.

Art, in all its forms, is simply a multifaceted form of communication. We are social beings. The sharing of stories increases public awareness of issues and events; provides social and political commentary; and validates the experiences of those who have witnessed or been part of similar stories.

Turbine

there is a machine that spins like a model of the universe, like a metal tornado, like a gyroscope made out of sign poles and loops of metal torn from smashing cars. it runs on sound, on the boom boom bass that you feel in your bones, the wall of silence of an impending storm. as it spins, its magnets shriek and crack, spitting sparks and generating an electric forcefield strong enough to blur your vision and bend the hairs on your arms. I want nothing more

than to be against you against this wall, against you against the wall. I bite my lip, turn my head away, bite the back of my hand to keep from screaming. a magnet pressed against a spine will rearrange neurons, realign fraying misfiring wires. breathe my words into the back of your neck. salt. scent of the ocean. I could lick you clean. we remember the taste of home. the hard shove

of horseshoe magnets negotiating, flip and smash into each other, a thin layer of skin caught between. your mouth moves. the taste of another's tongue. I cut my hands on your shoulderblades, cut my teeth on the edge of your smile. I want nothing more than to be against you against the wall, against you against the wall. I crack my skull

on your headboard, crack my teeth against yours, crack my knuckles to keep my hands to myself. the flash of metal past metal, bowed bands of steel and iron spinning into near-invisibility. we stand so close I can feel it in my bones. leave

my mark. territorial pissings. fingernail tattoos. mouth bruises. the soft give of flesh. I watch you

watching me. your skin smells like salt, like lightning, like a turbine spinning so hard so fast that it almost ceases to exist, blades passing so close that a copper penny would make it explode. the taste of your blood on my teeth keeps me hungry. the webbing of flesh between thumb and finger. magnets held on either side will snap together, will crush thin skin into pain, will lift the weight of anything worth holding on to. I want nothing more than to be against you. there is a machine that spins. it runs on sound and generates electricity. I want to stand against you against the wall, against you against the wall of forcefield magnetic electricity, press my hands to yours as though your bones were polarized metal and my blood were iron filaments. there is a machine that spins. it is bigger than both of us. we are constantly exploding with lightning.

JEN **CURRIN**

Jen Currin was born and raised in Portland, Oregon, and currently lives in Vancouver, BC. She teaches creative writing at Vancouver Film School and for Langara College's Continuing Studies program. A founding member of the poetry collective vertigo west, Jen has published two books of poems: *The Sleep of Four Cities* (Anvil Press, 2005) and *Hagiography* (Coach House, 2008).

I usually work as a sort of collagist, drawing from my own notebook and occasionally other sources. This poem, inspired by the paintings of Emily Church, was composed a bit differently. I sat in Emily's studio for a couple of hours looking closely at perhaps ten paintings and making several pages of notes about the images, as well as what they sparked in me (bits of narrative, color, etc.). Then I sat down with these notes and tried to find the poems in them — lines that stood out, seemed true, were connected to one another, etc. As I drafted, I made some changes, tightened things up, etc., and finally the poem(s) were done.

Black-Purple

Further into the dark forest
you disappear. Of course every tree
is half-human, which is why
their cries disturb us.
Why I must turn away
from this painting of a man's hip bones.

The birds miss them already.
Their absence a bruise.
You slip on ice at dusk & a blue tree stands up.
I know what you're thinking
& it's not from a photograph.
Shadows where trees once were,
the moon just outside the frame.
The few remaining leaves make a dry sound
in the wind.

We don't imagine them in purple light
but we are wrong.
Even my mother was once a tree.
A lonely white branch winking *Hello, Goodbye.*

The road is a scarf you wrap around them.
Someone kneels in the red grass.
The black trees are dead as snow.
Once I started drawing. You understand?
I started & I found night.

DANIELA **ELZA**

Daniela Bouneva Elza is working poetically on her Ph.D. in Philosophy of Education at SFU. Concurrently she is also working on her first poetry manuscript. Her work has appeared in *Existere, Quills, Paideusis, The Capilano Review, Contemporary Verse 2, Room of One's Own, The Arabesque Review, dANDelion*, and is forthcoming in *Educational Insights* and *Van Gogh's Ear*. She lives with her family in Vancouver.

I think of myself as a mapmaker, a kind of poesis-cartographer. Poems are the maps I offer as testimonies for places I have tried to explore, for what can be ascertained only through the footprints left by poems. I invite the reader onto these maps, to wander among, and through their landmarks, thought-marks. Not too well guided, I hope. But, not too lost. Yet, enough to discover something.

As a writer I am both interested in the process and the product. On the one hand the process of writing and mapping out the world I inhabit. What inhibits us from inhabiting better? On the other hand, as a reader I am curious how I can locate myself on another writer's map, and how that map serves as a point of departure. A place where writer and reader coexist in some whole and symbiotic relationship, where each benefits in surprising and unpredictable ways. Yet, each walks their own path. To enhance that, I experiment with form in the hope of offering a different experience of familiar words. I will never know how you read my poem. That is the beauty of it. That is a freedom we are entitled to as explorers of unexplored places.

The poem for me is the witnessing of a soul in its making, where it explores its world on the edge of the breath of another. That perfect moment where as an explorer, dreamer and maker I can hold your breath in forms. Where I invite readers to be the dreamer, the explorer and the maker. Where, with pure linguistic delight, we draw landscapes of mind with a cartographer's passion within, and beyond, the boundaries of our knowing.

* *quote in poem:* even the philosophy of metaphor is inescapably metaphorical.
– *K. Simms*

true	or false	(a triptych
in language) or false.	we become in metaphor	true (we encounter
the chaos) the flapping	ensuing of a wing	from in the east.
stirring thought	a tornado science—	Nietzsche *the cemetery*
of perception.	Neil Bohr	saw the atom
as a drop *the philosophy*	of water. *of metaphor*	*even* *is inescapably* *metaphorical*
to define it we can	is . to . see get to	how close a bird
before it takes off.		the measurement
irrelevant.	the pursuit in (the mouth	left open.)

MONA **FERTIG**

Mona Fertig is a poet, book artist and publisher. She opened The Literary Storefront in Gastown in 1978. In its heyday it had 500 members and readings every week. It was the birthplace of the Federation of BC Writers and housed the first regional TWUC office. Her books and chapbooks of poetry include: *Sex Death & Travel, This is Paradise* and *Invoking the Moon.* She edited *A Labour of Love,* an anthology of poetry on pregnancy and childbirth. She helped initiate the Dorothy Livesay Prize for Poetry and was the BC/Yukon Rep for the Writers' Union of Canada and PEN Canada. She runs Mother Tongue Publishing on Salt Spring Island.

I have always written poetry and always will. There is a layer of our lives that needs watering with poetry. Deep down. It connects us to what is past and what is coming. Unknown. Archetypal. Unspoken. Old as dreams.

Poetry should be read on street corners, hung on banners in cities, cited in soccer stadiums, at political meetings, work and in schools. After gardening and your throat is parched, words go well with wine.

Poetry is a vibration that can shimmy open the doors to inner and outer truths, ushering in a sweet silence … after an epiphany sneaks through.

Year of the Dog

In the village the air is steely grey, *stores vacant, sales down,*
rents high, the whimpering has begun,

the face of winter lingers despite the lengthening hours,
even the stout unshaven farmers rarely come to town,

spit on the barn floor, shovel shit, shear sheep,
delouse the chickens, sell eggs – $4.50 a dozen,

chop wood, empty the honour box, huddle with their dogs in pickups,
forge in Fulford, North End road.

When they venture to town for supplies
they pull in for apple pie and coffee, *lunch at Dagwoods*

or a Chinese special at the Golden Island,
their trusty mutts happily guarding the truck

sit in the driver's seat, faces like friends.
This new year is mild until a cold snap,

when the sun finally shoots through skylights,
it uplifts yearning bulbs, *daffodils bloom*.

What will the Year of the Dog bring? *Loyalty?*
People shopping locally? Housing for the working poor?

Or a continual exodus off-island for better housing, box stores,
a 5-day school week?

Camellia's false exuberance spreads against old farmhouses,
lipstick on a tired septuagenarian, clumps of snowdrops cluster,

pups eager for a patch of March sun.
2006. *A handlick, a belly rub, or a bite?*

The pack, *unthinking*, ready to turn or lunge at the scent of sheep or fear.
Alpha dog unyielding?

Top dog takes all?
Only the good bitch knows.

GEORGE **FETHERLING**

George Fetherling is the author of eleven poetry collections and chapbooks, including a *Selected Poems* (1994) and the long poem *Singer, An Elegy* (2004). In all, he has published fifty books of fiction, history, biography, travel and cultural commentary. He lives in the West End of Vancouver, within sight of the Sylvia Hotel.

Somewhere in one of his wonderful essays, Kenneth Rexroth wrote that when the African-American musicians of New Orleans moved up the Mississippi River to Chicago in the early twentieth century, they were also moving, inevitably, inexorably, from blues to jazz, much as the Russian intelligentsia, following the failed revolution of 1905, went from naturalism to the occult. These were both cases, Rexroth continued, of artists seeking out a new language that the cops couldn't understand. To me, this points up one of the great utilities of poetry as well, as least in the ways I struggle to use the form: to communicate with the readers directly but in a kind of exalted code that evades both third-party eavesdropping.

I Call To The Windows

I call to the windows
to witness the way I decode
the new language of your laughter.
Stand ready to be surprised, I say
almost daring events to unravel.

My thoughts enunciate sharply
what you do not wish to hear.
One day speech will slip out.
It just got away from me somehow, officer,
like a renegade whipsaw.
I understand.
                    You understand
that the worst is not over
the worst has yet to exhaust itself
in the legacy of old desires
kept folded in wallets or hidden in picture frames
deposited with bankers in Amsterdam
who know all about the utility of secrets
and how to work the system for everything it's worth.

Your absence is my only landmark.
With that and a loonie I can get a coffee.
With that, a compass and a wristwatch
I can't possibly get lost.
On the map my dilemma looks like an accident.

So I walk to the rim of the city
(this takes longer than it used to)
and find that the prairie is still there
beneath the need and the sky.
The lights are like confetti when I
look back, the lies like litter
at my feet.

MARYA **FIAMENGO**

Marya Fiamengo was born in 1926 in Vancouver, BC, the child of immigrants from the Croatian island of Vis. She earned a Bachelor's Degree in English from UBC and a Master's Degree in English and Creative Writing under the direction of Earle Birney and Dorothy Livesay. She taught in the English Dept at UBC from 1962-1993, publishing seven volumes of poetry as well as numerous critical reviews and essays. Since the early 1970s she has been a passionate advocate of Canadian culture and national autonomy. She lives in Gibsons, BC. *Visible Living: Poems Selected and New*, was published in 2006 by Ronsdale Press.

I write inspired by what delights or pains me: manifestations of the Divine on the rare occasions these occur. Nature, of course, the beauty of landscape, the power of wilderness. Human history past and present; the past is often more alive for me than the problematical present.

My poems explore the often painful labyrinth of my Slavic ancestry. I am receptive to most things Slavic: Russia's tragic politics, Poland's pain, the colours of Ukraine, Czech and Slovak particularities; but, most of all, whatever pertains to the late Socialist Republic of Yugoslavia whose demise was a personal painful heartbreak. My parents were from the island of Vis in the Adriatic Sea, perhaps one of the most beautiful seas in the world.

I am intransigently Euro-Centric. I regard, "touchy-feely" liberalism as a cancer in the body politic. Sappho, Plato and Euripedes speak to me in a way nothing else, not even Rumi or Confucius do.

Lastly, I am a feminist, albeit a mild one, I have difficulties with societies which oppress women. What matters in the end is whatever affirms the validity, integrity and sanctity of the human spirit. This is what poetry does. "All Art," the French poet Mallarmé writes, "aspires to the condition of music." Poetry is the music of language.

Reflections on Vladimir Putin at Prayer

One murky evening
in the early twenty-first century
watching the evening news
I saw Vladimir Putin
former Head of the NKVD now President
of Russia kneeling reverently
before the coffin of Marya Feodorovna
the late Czar Nicholas II's grandmother.

Above him the Metropolitan of
the Russina Orthodox Church
intoned the luminous liturgy
            of the Requiem Mass.
Putin devoutly and correctly
at the appropriate moment
made the Orthodox sign of the Cross.
The sacramental cadence of the
funeral music poured out of
the newscast, Canada's CBC
at its very best.

I sat transfixed in a historical trance.
Marya Feodorovna, Empress of all the Russias,
brought home to rest at the personal
intercession of none other than
Gospodin Vladimir Putin once, no doubt,
committed Marxist materialist, now
found at prayer.

In that bitter-sweet moment
The labyrinthian bells of painful
Russian history rang their astonished
question in my ears.
Shto Vladimir, Shto eto ?
What does this mean?
Is it atonement for Ekaterinburg ?

Or a deft Byzantine gesture
of political expediency?

As I gaze at your set inscrutable
face a frantic hope
stirs in my heart.

Of course, there are those in the liberal democratic west
who regard you as a thug.
And assuredly it may not be
possible to make it big
in the NKVD with kid gloves.

But are you any the worse than George Bush?
Or the corporate capitalist class
which will sanitize any number of atrocities
to protect economic securities.

While you are not entirely
my line of country, au fond
I prefer impassioned Pushkin,
damaged Doestoevsky and testy
towering Tolstoy; yet I warm
to you for in this winter
of my declining years as I
listen to the indestructible
harmonies that pushed back
the Tartar hordes at Kazan
and endorsed the stubborn matchless
courage of Stalingrad.
I say yes.
However, unlikely or improbable
yes to the possibility of
the miraculous and see
in my mind's eye
sudden and unexpected
Mimosa blooming in the Russian snow.

CATHY **FORD**

Poet, fictioniste, memoirist, writer of long poems, creative non-fiction, language-centred feminist. Published: *Stray Zale, the murdered dreams awake, Tall Trees, Blood Uttering, The Desiring Heart, Affaires of the Heart, By Violent Means, the womb rattles its pod poems, Saffron, Rose & Flame - the joan of arc poems, Cunnilingus* or *How I Learned to Love Figure Skating, Sexing the Angels,* and others. Born Saskatchewan, grew-up in northern BC, UBC BFA and MFA with Honours. Presently League of Canadian Poets Access Copyright representative. A founder of the LCP Feminist Caucus. Forthcoming: editor of feminist theory and eroticism poetics chapbooks in Living Archives Series.

A bead necklace on poetics, actualized, looked for in poems, conscious with, contained in, clear about, cognizant of, art pieces made of words, gifts… acuity, allegory, art, angels, awe, alphabet, ability, ambition, artists, awareness – beauty, brilliance, burning, billetdoux, birthing, bear, bare, bones - compassion, conviction, consciousness, culture, creativity, charcoal, comment, comprehension, children, crow, coincidence, ceremony, courage, changing the world, clarity, challenge, colour, complexity, creativity, candling – deconstruction, death, desire, depth, design, difference, domesticity, drawing, distinction, drowning, delicacy - enjambment, eroticism, ecstasy, examination, emancipation, ethos, excerpts, experimentation, eagle, embroidery, education - faith, feminism, fertility, flight, form, flowers, fiction, five senses, flames, fiduciary responsibility, fire - giftedness, grace, goddessness, gardens, generosity, genius, grief - humility, humanism, handwork, hummingbirds, handwriting, history – intent, imagination, incarnation, impatience, integrity, intensity, innocence, impressions, interface, inspiration, intelligence, image – justice, jazz, journals – killerwhales, kineticism - labryrinthicism, love, lyricism, linguistics, landscape, literature, languagecentred, light, luminosity, letters- music, marriage, memory, mars, memoirism, myth, metaphor, mirroring, modernism, man, metamorphosis - narrative, nature, nouns, nakedness - originality, orchidaciousness – sometimes through tall grass, water's edge, that creature whose skin is the same colour as its stripes, zebra.

* lyrics in poem from traditional gospel spirituals, songs for peace; remark from Georgia O'Keefe, painter.

Just Kissing Paradise Goodbye

Flat black the sea at Odessa
awaiting summer, edge of the sea heavy as frantic immigration
Russian iron crosses in Swedish country, on Granville, at Vancouver
ask yourself where have you been where have you come from

bound leather books as storage cases, including the long married faithful
memoirist Tess of the d'Urbervilles, embroidered clothes of the disappearing
endangered species swept off the face of the earth, and War and Peace
"free at last free at last freedomland. . . last night I dreamed the strangest dream"

just after facing down an end to war, time flies, death bird's cannibal cry,
wings spread
ghosted Bella Pacifica, summer 1992 or was it 1994, first totem animal gone
raven crow like Icarus, my crow is dead mommy my crow
my son weeping

pounding the wood semaphore for grief cross into the sand
I hold him, never let go, alive or living still inside each of us
always he will return to this place, you also
the child who cannot forget

"artists should sew their mouths shut"

years later, August 2007, reed wrapped talisman Christ shaped crucifix fell
from the sky, found at rest, resurrection, on the same beach log he'd carved
his life into
then he survived

> head on collision
> road to Tofino
> past midnight
> road back
> our son

we were waiting for the cell phone to ring, in our smoky very frail bones
his father and… I was already stunned silent

where are you he said where are you when he called

DAVID **FRASER**

David Fraser lives in Nanoose Bay on Vancouver Island. He is the founder and editor of Ascent Aspirations Magazine, since 1997. His poetry and short fiction have appeared in over 50 journals and anthologies. He has published a collection of his poetry, *Going to the Well* (2004), a collection of short fiction, *The Dark Side of the Billboard* (2006) and a second collection of poetry, *Running Down the Wind* (2007). He is currently the Federation of BC Writers Regional Director for The Islands Region. His latest passion is developing Nanaimo's newest spoken-word series, WordStorm, www.wordstorm.ca

Much has been said about why poetry in its many forms has become marginalized in western society. Poetry is just one of the victims in a hurried world that favours consumerism and profits as an expression of its culture.

Despite the fact that more is happening with poetry – spoken word events, slams, a proliferation of ezines, small press electronic sites, personal web pages, more local readings, and more poetry books being published – poetry, in the wider sense of western culture, is not valued, possibly because it doesn't generate wealth, add to the gross national product or reach the mainstream audiences of our society.

In his poem, "Ozymandias," Shelley explores many great themes, such as arrogance and the transience of influence and power. The "two vast and trunkless legs of stone" are all that remain of the great king and his great kingdom. Ironically, Shelley's poem remains. There is permanence in real art, and the poetry, songs, and other artistic expressions of a society although not so valued as the towering monuments to power, are in fact what remain of value after a civilization has long departed. Just ask any archaeologist.

Finding a Path
An Epiphany

Staring at the portrait mirror
silver backing freckled off
above the basement laundry tubs
where we washed our hair,
I knew.
I just knew after watching you
come home one night
wearing work upon your skin,
shiny pant-smell of
diesel on your hands, the coarse-
woven collar of your uniform
turned up against what all
the world could throw at you,
or rain down on you,
for it had to be a rainy night
when looking in that mirror,
my face not yet nearly out of school,
I knew, I just knew,
though not a stranger to hard work,
I'd find a path that didn't
bring me home at night
that way.

PATRICK **FRIESEN**

Patrick Friesen writes poetry, drama, scripts, essays, song lyrics, and text for dance and music. He has won the McNally Robinson Book of the Year Award in Manitoba, and been shortlisted for the Governor General's Award for Poetry and twice for the BC Book Awards. Friesen has produced two spoken word/improv music CDs with Marilyn Lerner. His most recent books have been *Interim: Essays & Mediations* (Hagios, 2006) and *Earth's Crude Gravities* (Harbour, 2007).

I'd rather listen to a song than a lecture. It's not that I don't enjoy a good lecture, but it usually has a fairly limited life, both in content and impact. The song goes deeper and lasts longer. It resonates, keeps rising to the surface of consciousness. It's always there. I hear it when my mother remembers a passage of poetry from her grade school days, or she sings a song learned in childhood. I've read about it in Evgenia Ginzburg's books about life in Stalinist camps; the act of remembering poetry she had never intentionally memorized often kept her alive as a human being.

The physical world is our existence now; all meaning arises viscerally, suggestively, from this. And there is the sound of language on human tongues. Inarticulation moving toward understanding. Air taken into our lungs — spirit, keeping us alive — then moving out across vocal cords, past palate, tongue, teeth and lips. Astonishingly, we have learned to shape breath, to speak and sing. There should be rituals to celebrate this. And, perhaps, that is one of the things poetry does.

I'll say that an emerging poem gives me the same excitement, alertness, the same pleasure as I experience upon seeing an animal step into a clearing. There is that kind of wildness about it.

gone like the bell-ringer's wife

gone like the bell-ringer's wife like the voice in the garden gone like the good
ships and fair winds
how long since you've tasted your shadow licking it where it lingers on the white
stucco wall
and how long gone the story of old days your mother told before bedtime the
story of the drowned sailor

the storm was rolling in and gods were weeping did we hear that sound the gods
were leaving earth
did we hear the door close the blue door at the top of the steps did we hear our
rude words to the strangers
we turned from them the wind riding through willows through the orchard
shaking drunken fruit to the ground

sometimes we thought we heard them talking faintly as if through a veil words
at the root of us
sometimes we ran across paths that were still warm animal or god it was always
hard to know
and when the world went silent for a while we asked the band to strike up we
learned not to whisper

everything sank beneath the sea the silver spears and buckles the basins and the
banquet bowls
islands swamped one by one the islands inside disappeared leaving nothing but
summer and flotsam behind
and people prayed with thick tongues they worshipped like cattle bawling in the
noonday heat

did we see her lying beneath the wreckage of her dress on her elbows and
arching her back
always there was night at the stream's mouth and a way through night the seed
dropping into the rift
the bell tolled three times the rope uneasy as the bell-ringer dragged his feet
toward his empty house

COLIN **FULTON**

Colin Fulton is twenty-one and currently studies creative writing at the University of Victoria. He was born in Calgary, but raised during the school year in Nova Scotia with his mother as summers were spent in the Okanagan with his father. At the age of eighteen Colin moved permanently to British Columbia to pursue his writing, and took a year off to backpack throughout South America. Colin currently makes his home in Victoria.

I grew up in Nova Scotia but now live in Victoria, and no decision I've made in my life has rung more correctly than choosing to move to the West Coast from the East. There are palatable differences between how both the Pacific and the Atlantic enter my writing: varying saltiness, warmth, tidal flux. All of these are obnoxious metaphors I know, but they seem apt to me. I feel that I'll always need to live in close proximity to the ocean — and of course mountains. Discovering the beauty of Vancouver Island's unison of those two was like seeing a painting of myself made before I was born. Opposing philosophies, environments and personalities are always going to inform me at the very roots of my art. Poetry in Canada – particularly in British Columbia – has always been ready to reach into its wilderness and frontier mentality for content, and with great style and beauty. It seems that what I'm reading now in BC poetry continues to strike down its nature writing stereotype with new approaches to the natural, but I think as a whole our province is finding a voice beyond that with surprising strength and multiplicity. My piece here is not obviously "nature poetry," but still explores natural themes. It subconsciously owes everything to the juxtaposition of East and West that I reconcile every day as a person, and it has a strong narrative, which I've developed a taste for after living inside all of BC's untold stories. When the environment of a place changes as ours continues to, then so will the words that come from its writers.

Vancouver

There's a body here.   This night on call
found a ragdoll flung from its fibreglass trap: her,
Jeep Cherokee roll bar frame torn up, boyfriend dead.
We swung oxygen censers wide and steady – monks
above her one ripe lip. I peeled painted cloth from skin
and hair platinum-blonde made red. Black lipstick mouths
a moan now. Her stare returns. There is mist.

Scent comes of dried kelp and cheap burnt dahl, ocean's heard
at the bottom of Vine; this hour of overtime is worth 30.65.
Gauze arches go around her temples, we unfold her,
I clasp shut each cut embossed by the curb.
She has been others, she has been here
where welts sunrise.

Our cab is full with her erratic heartbeat morse and I
only accelerate past each downtown corner watching
yield,   stop,   merge signs pass by. Spatters of people
sprawl in a sprawling town. Pay no mind to the ambulance:
we're free from your kind of physics.

I am seeing what this girl did not in the kinetic steepness
of streets. Weaving;
our siren a needle, this city at the water's hem.

CARLA **FUNK**

Carla Funk was born and raised amidst logging trucks and Mennonites in Vanderhoof, BC. After high school, she moved to Victoria and earned degrees in Writing and English Literature at UVic. Since then, her work has been featured in various anthologies including *Breathing Fire: Canada's Young Poets* (Harbour, 1995), and in Canadian literary journals. She has published three collections of poetry: *Blessing the Bones into Light* (Coteau Books, 1999); *Head Full of Sun* (Nightwood Editions, 2002); and *The Sewing Room* (Turnstone Press, 2006). She now lives in Victoria with her husband and daughter, where she teaches in UVic's Department of Writing, and in 2008 is the City's inaugural poet laureate.

All through my childhood, my mother saved worn dresses, stained blue jeans and outgrown clothes. She'd cut the material into squares and sew patchwork blankets. My grandmother kept fabric scraps – even her old underwear – to make braided rugs. Weekly, my grandpa checked the town dump for garbage that was too good to throw away – a lopsided tricycle, a tea kettle, a lamp without its shade. In poetry, I find I'm saving scraps, cutting away from memory what's useful, picking through the cast-offs. More and more, I'm seeing the redemptive urge of poetry, how it wants to turn junk into beauty, to sift through the ash-heap for a piece of broken glass to hold up and catch the light.

Highway 16 Sonnet

—for Donna Kane

I walked all summer long a stretch of road
known by locals as a risk. Trucks flew past,
(the posted speed limit a joke) loaded
up with wood, junk, flammables, and fastened
to the gas. Every week, at least one new
creature hit the ditch or shoulder, was hit
and hurled, fur and blood, next to some lost shoe
or bottle in shards. I counted on it,
needed that mess of beauty to send me
back to the empty room with something to say.
Dog, cat, rabbit, squirrel, fox, crow – debris
of a wilder gutted kingdom, decaying
with the kind of grace I've come to envy –
honest, splayed out for the world to see.
That kind of death I understand. Easy.
It's the other I can't take, the in-between,
like the doe that waited on the roadside
for her wobbling fawn with its wrecked backbone
and muzzle dripping red. It struggled, tried
to walk, fell down. I kept moving towards home
where the page waited. You know how it goes.
Words faltered, dragged, then from the dirt, they rose.

MAXINE **GADD**

Born in England during the Battle of Britain, 1940. Migrated to Hardesty, Alberta in 1946. Vancouver 1947. Six years at Kitsilano High when Beatnikism arrived. Went to black light cafés in Dunbar and Kits, steamy old European cafés on Robson Street. Graduated from UBC with a BA and a baby in 1962. Published by bill bissett's, blewointment press and Bertrand Lachance, air press. Edited by Daphne Marlatt and Ingrid Klassen for Coach House Press, *Lost Language*, 1982. (m)Öthêr Tøñgué Presš, *Fire in the Cove*, 2001. Recently published by New Star Books, *Backup to Babylon,* 2007 (nominated for the Dorothy Livesay prize), and *Subway Under Byzantium*, 2008. A third much hoped for book is perhaps being born in the Great Chaos. The poems presently surround me, waiting like angelic genii in the dark. Or are they mice being eaten by words? Or just tales?

All human languages and likely those of other species have grammatical rules and variations. A young person in Haida, Cree, Zulu, Parsi, Seung Hoi, Francaise anywhere on earth or in time will be able to say to a new friend just learning their language, some equivalent of "We tend to capitalize proper names or it's just not cool to do so, identity being such a predetermined concept; if we want to be respected by some people say ain't; or for civil servants and teachers we say, "Are not, or aren't." This "aren't" was in my school days considered incorrect though it persisted into usage.

We are all intensely aware of correctness, connectiveness and structure and many of us rebel, *epater le bourgeois et las bourgeoisie*, get in yr face, say why or why not. All languages have poetries and poetics and experts and mavens. All poetries have song or anti-song, mnemonics for legends, muses, djinns, the miraculous, the matter-of-fact and foolery, intricate or plain, and we all practice stitches, weavings, enchantment, truth, anti-truth, functional mathematics, negative functions and justice. Variation is our delight. And monotony, metonymy leading to MMMMMNNNeMMMMMNN the chant of insects and ghosts, horror, history, infamy and praise. We hate and adore our tongues, twist them, turn them, indulge their perversions; shout for strait forms like stiletto heels and corsets, cripple our bodies and ... any day now I will feel myself called upon to produce a sonnet.

Anyhow

well there's less lying around being specious
that was then
blank shhheet it
starts
in its own
drone
and with a howl i join my daemon
returning through one of a thousand doors
but
being no other
no bother
Sure, Miss, but the twit is quite its other
kernels no end of smart art corn/being born and grown takes faith
below fair
bowel-red painted wooden bowl.

So, my souls we tarry in our tavern, rejoice, argue, quarrel
We kill ourselves and our friends do themselves in
kill relatives
but slowly over ninety-nine decades we stride across the sky
in boots made of butterfly wings

something
sustains us
briefly
lightly

we sit in pubs where there's only men
and the women who serve them

PAM **GALLOWAY**

Born in northern England, Pam Galloway now lives in Vancouver. She has worked as a freelance writer, creative writing instructor and speech and language therapist. Her poetry is published in numerous anthologies and literary magazines. She contributed to the collection *Quintet – Themes and Variations* along with four other poets (Ekstasis Editions, 1998). Her first solo book was *Parallel Lines* (Ekstasis Editions, 2006). Through 2007-2009, her poetry will be included in the Poetry in Transit project. In May 2008 she was awarded a high commendation in the Petra Kenney poetry competition (UK/Canada collaboration). She has an MFA in creative writing from UBC.

I began to pay attention to poems as an infant. My mother's bed-time "stories" were more often told through songs and poems. The threads of connection between song, the music of poetry and the webs of story were drawn through me and sewn in place as my mother recited rhymes and poems and sang to me the old songs. She learned the poetry of Victorian England by heart and gave it to me as she sat on my bed each night. She would move from Blake's somewhat ominous " Tyger " on to faster paced poems like R.L. Stevenson's "From a Railway Carriage" with its train-on-the-tracks rhythm and then wind her way toward the lullabies. I lay, eyelids drooping, as I drifted to places I could barely imagine and would surely never visit. I absorbed into my developing sense of self a deep appreciation of rhythm and rhyme, of stories told in condensed and yet magnificently detailed forms. And now, I try to achieve something of the same by writing poetry.

I write in response to the world I inhabit and to the small, and sometimes not so small, losses that are a natural part of existence. In my poems I try to encapsulate vital details, whether these are of a changing landscape or some aspect of human connection. I forget which wise poet said that all poetry is about loss; that in writing a poem the poet is engaged in an effort to recapture something that has passed. In this, poetry must always fail. If this is true, then poetry is an aspect of human endeavour which makes something meaningful and lasting out of failure.

Inside this house

The hum and whirr of the wood-chip stove
pushes cold air back into the reaches
of the kitchen, toward the door
that will not fully close (ridiculous
on this first January day, ten below
and threatening colder) while waves of warmth
roil along the corridor into bedrooms,
more welcoming now they're lived in,
cluttered and strewn with blankets,
discarded clothing, half-emptied travel-bags.

Outside, stark branches scratch at
a snow-swollen sky like fingertips
searching out an entry-point to heaven.
The window frames a silvered birch, its branches
high above; its trunk could be the supporting beam
of a grander house: that sky, the bloodless walls,
alabaster ceiling – unimaginable
it could ever break, ever be broken.
Planes, missiles, bombs – all are un-invented
as I wait for night to slide
its thickly-gloved fingers over my eyes

LORRAINE **GANE**

Lorraine Gane's essays, articles, reviews and poetry have been published widely in magazines, journals and newspapers across Canada, the US and Britain. She has taught writing at such venues as Ryerson, McMaster and the University of Victoria, as well as private workshops across Canada and online courses to students across North America. Among her poetry collections are *Earth Light, Even the Slightest Touch Thunders on My Skin* and *The Phantom Orchid*. She is working on several other writing projects.

Over the last fifteen years my aim as a poet has been to write about the place where the ordinary and the extraordinary meet. My first opportunity to practice the deep seeing required in such work was during the writing of a collection of poems about the illness and death of my fiancé from cancer in the early and mid `90s. Nearing the completion of *Even the Slightest Touch Thunders on My Skin*, I was increasingly drawn to the natural world to deepen my explorations. On my walks into the forests and other undisturbed places of Salt Spring Island, I began to sense the deep imprints in the land, not only its physical components, but also its mythological and historical undercurrents. This was reflected in the poems that began emerging about the natives who lived on the island before the white settlers arrived. My interest, then, became telling the legends and stories that seemed hidden in the landscape and yet a very real part of its living presence. I began to see that these poems were part of a larger work called *The Dreaming Songs*, which explores not only the deep layers of specific places on the West Coast, but also the interconnectedness of all places. To do this, the poems use linking devices such as the four natural elements of water, air, earth and fire.

Autumn Rains

1

In the forest
white caps ignite a dark sea
and as the weeks go by
skins split apart at the edges
torn ragged like flowers,
yet among the sweet decay
a red skull appears
etched with a loosely drawn "Y,"
perhaps for "Yield,"
or maybe "Yes, Yes, Yes!"

2

Darkness,
this room quiet tonight,
my heart still
in the shudder of rain.

3

This morning
a new appearance on the fallen fir—
tongues of translucent gel,
springy to my touch
and Thoreau's words come back to me
from a time before speed was everything:
We must know what we want;
How much is enough?

4

The rains have stopped,
blue sky above the tops of trees
and in this morning light
puff balls spring up in milky pods,
white lace dresses the forest floor,
such growth in the month of death,
underground the earth alive with spores,
and some heaviness lifts,
the song the stream makes
a soft bell that plays continuously,
ocean in the bell
and all the streams like this one
sounding too.
Without darkness, we wouldn't see the light.
Our lives pass through us to the other side
where we cannot reach them,
every breath taking us there.
Slowly.

RHONDA **GANZ**

Born in Kenya, Rhonda Ganz moved to BC in 1980. In 2006, she was a finalist in *The Malahat Review's Far Horizons Poetry Award,* and in 2007, the CBC broadcast one of her poems as part of National Poetry Month. Friday nights find her reading and listening at Planet Earth Poetry in Victoria. When not working as a graphic designer and editor, she paints botanical watercolours and reads too much crime fiction.

I want my poetry to revel in rhyme and tattle and the percussion of words strung together in palpable rhythm — with enough of a story to propel the reader or the listener through to the end. A twist, a provocation, a frisson of revulsion, are not unwelcome. Poems scramble logic. A proper sequence of events is not essential to poetry. My poems examine the small moments, the pith, of intimacy and domesticity. Nature, when present, is secondary to human characters and relationships. I will never cease to be fascinated by the way people behave, and to mine my inspiration from love and argument. Performance alters a poem. I consider how a poem will sound off the page as well as when read quietly in the mind. Part of the fun of reading out loud is playing with modulation, with pauses, with how fast or slow certain lines are read — no poem is ever the same twice. Poetry started with oral presentation of song and story, and in Victoria the tradition of poets reading or reciting poems to each other, whether at open mike or at spoken word events, is a tradition I am delighted to be a part of.

You can take the girl out of the city

This doorknob   does not want to be a no need for deadbolt doorknob on the door
to paint peeled wind flecked one room shed in slumber field at the
end of no go nowhere gravel road.

This doorknob wants to unlock room dirty bedspread 53
at past its prime lovers flop box on the corner of what am I doing
in this part of town and gotta gun in my pocket—wants to
wonder what was on the hand of booze on his breath stumble
needs a shave—wants to wait for smells pretty gum chewy
Fondala Gondala fingernails to grab hold and take a turn.

This piece of plywood   does not want to be the splinter warp splittery gouge flake
edge doesn't fit right cover to hey at least we're on septic
hits bedrock too soon spider bucket boondocks well.

This plywood wants to be a section of peep through a hole
soggy empty lot hoarding in no place is safe neighbourhood
—wants to tempt skate racer spray can neon slogan punk ass tagger
—wants to sloppy glue handbill big font rock band poster poster
Wet Guitar and the Look-Alikes slap it up take it down.

This chair   does not want to be fresh paint smell coffee cooling
on the armrest Adirondack above the tide line on it's so quiet
you can hear yakety-yak what the hell is that bird called
all the way across the bay it's why we moved here beach.

This chair wants to lean back on fixer upper saggy porch
at the top of wobbly stairs on still a bit dicey street
—wants wine oopsy spill on creaky seat from jump up and kiss me
honey you're home—wants to invite hi there Mrs. Paxton never
scoops poop yippy-yap to homemade chocolate chip cookie
stop and take a load off.

This piece of glass   does not want to be smooth sand rubbed edge green in artsy-fartsy
beachcomber seashell barnacle collage look how pretty wormy
sandflea let's sit here sandy dampy driftwood shit my pants are wet.

This glass wants to be smash wall shatter sharp back alley
bar door open two men fight fight isn't it always bloody bricks
about the girl—wants to be city park duck pond green water
bobbing bottle stone throwing boy target—wants dawn break
sun sliver gutter glimmer got laid last night whistle
streetsweeper twirly brush to take it for a tumble.

Oh my doorknob, oh my plywood, oh my chair
oh cut my heart out shard of glass

At midnight I will pack you in the back of but sugar we need
a four wheel drive out here—deliver you from bucolic sweetgrass
goose honk wind chime birdsong soggy wet wood smokey
blister finger branches falling windstorm no backup generator
no bars cell phone forget about fucking wireless backwoods
backwater.

This girl's gonna ditch her rustic frolic, this girl so wants back
to bright light big box open late lurchy bus people shout car siren
city siren three a.m. car car six screen butter popcorn new release
people people busker nightschool swim class take-out pizza art
show book club bike lane Chinatown wants to sit down Friday
night half-caf latte frothy lip foam run mouth poet in every chair
at the open mike read to me   read to me   read to me café.

HEIDI **GARNETT**

Heidi Garnett began writing five years ago when she retired from teaching and began to study with John Lent. Since then she has been published in a variety of literary journals including *Event, CV2, Antigonish Review, Arc, New Quarterly, Room,* etc. Her first book of poetry was published in 2006 by Thistledown Press. She has placed in the Shuswap Writer's Festival, poetry and fiction prize, 2004, 2005, Arc Poem of Year 2006, Great Blue Heron Contest, 2007. She's been accepted to the Banff Centre three times to work with poets Tim Lilburn, Don McKay, Tim Bowling and Anne Simpson and has been a student of Patrick Lane's. Fall 2008 she will be attending UBC in the Masters of Fine Arts program with Sharon Thesen as advisor.

Forgetting remembers itself into poems, images like birds tied by the thinnest strings to our fingers, that unconscious tugging. Recently, during a meditation I realized young aspects of myself had flown away because of traumatic events witnessed as a child. I visualized those fragile beings as birds, just specks in the sky, and although I had no conscious memory of them, they were still connected to me by strings. For me, each poem is like one of those birds, hardly visible, hardly believable, the way they hover at the edge of understanding, yet once they're grounded by words, they become more real and revealing than we ever imagined. Such is the power of poetry. This remembering of ourselves. This remembering of each other. This remembering of our world.

Free Range

Cattle kneeled in the night field
mouths stuffed with twice eaten grass,
sere, bitter. In April,
when they were driven down from the hills,
they bawled and milled about, stared big eyed at each other
as if they'd forgotten how to graze fenced land,
stand in such close proximity to houses
and humans. On the open range
they wander the eye's field,
the hilly terrain of instinct,
follow light's circadian patterns. After dark
they shelter in pine copses dazed with green dreaming,
stars. Tonight,
a sky windowless as an abattoir,
a pasture that imposes its own rhythms.
You feel like lying down with them
mindless as chewing, empty as outline,
to live in the world as if you've never loved
or been forgiven. What lies ahead of you
bone white and alphabetical,
already written. The grass
quick and silver now, moon glazed,
the pelt of some small frightened animal
caught in a leg hold trap
gnawing its way free.

GARY **GEDDES**

Gary Geddes was born in Vancouver and now divides his time between Victoria and French Beach. He has published and edited more than thirty-five books and won more than a dozen national and international literary awards, including the Gabriela Mistral Prize (Chile), Poetry Book Society Recommendation (UK) and the Lt-Governor's Award for Literary Excellence (British Columbia). His recent titles include *Sailing Home: A Journey Through Time, Place & Memory, Skaldance, Kingdom of Ten Thousand Things: An Impossible Journey from Kabul to Chiapas* and *Falsework,* all of which appeared on bestseller lists in Canada.

A visit to the cemetery in Venice to pay my respects at the grave of Ezra Pound resulted in several surprises. First, for a poet who took great pains to be exact and particular in his art, Pound's grave was overgrown and decidedly unkempt. Second, despite being a recluse in his final years, he was now sharing the Venetian afterlife with two flamboyant and irascible predecessors, Igor Stravinsky and Sergei Diaghelev. However, my biggest surprise was finding the grave of yet another Russian, Joseph Brodsky, the most recent newcomer. By contrast, Brodsky's tomb was extremely well-groomed and sporting considerable evidence of frequent visitors. It was these little tribute items, left behind by his friends and admirers that caught my attention and triggered the writing of "Vodorosli."

Intimate details, that's where most of my poems begin. A story told to me about a botched interview with a veteran in a Manitoba wheat field led to the writing of *Hong Kong Poems.* Four small details about Sandra Lee Scheuer (she was a speech therapy student, very tidy, non-political and liked to roller skate), found in a book by I. F. Stone, enabled me to write a poem (an elegy, as it turned out) that I'd been struggling with for five years about the killings at Kent State University. A newspaper anecdote about Paul Joseph Chartier, the so-called mad bomber of the House of Commons, led to the writing of *War & Other Measures.* As John Berger so rightly observes: "Poetry makes language care because it renders everything intimate. . . . There is nothing more substantial to place against the cruelty and indifference of the world than this caring."

Vodorosli

for Joseph Brodsky

Late morning, little traffic, Venetian crows soft-pedalling
in the ornamental cedars, Adriatic cul-de-sac.
Brodsky at rest, passport in order, papers in the archive.
His grave's a mess from all the visitors. A mandala

dangles from the headstone by a leather cord.
Beside the slab a flask of vodka, half empty, and
a little plastic pail of ball-point pens. A dozen roses
with a business-card, signed: Mr. X, Collector

of Fine Art, phone number in New York. No judges
here or KGB to label him a parasite. After watching
Visconti's *Death in Venice,* Brodsky dreamt of ending it
on a San Marco waterway, using, with all due irony,

a Browning revolver. Instead of dying in Venice,
he did the next best thing, took out permanent residence.
He had his favourites. Pound wasn't one, despite
translations and a shared enthusiasm

for 'making it new.' They'd never met, only Olga,
keeper of the flame, toeing the party-line: no fascism,
no anti- Semitism. Ezra's a Jewish name, she argued.
Neighbours now, not rivals, Joseph the new kid

on the block. Beauty: a stay against forgetting,
loss, the illusion of its timelessness. Venice, he said
in *Watermark*, dissolves the self. It's palazzi with their
portraits, putti and porphyry: sunken treasures

best viewed underwater, eyes wide, mouth shut tight.
The latter mode proved difficult: a hectoring teacher,
confrontational, dismissive, all that bluster to keep at bay
the self-disgust and insecurities of youth, the tortured

English, a struggle even Stockholm could not cure.
I recall his observation that the end of illness is the end
of metaphor. He'd been writing about Susan Sontag,
their visit to Olga, the Gaudier-Brzeska bust of Pound

nearby, Susan with her cancer, Joseph fighting
(discarded cigarette filters notwithstanding) heart disease.
A touching moment, two naked selves eroding, swathed
in history, both present, both departed. What goings-on

these ball-point pens would tell us if they could.
I bring the smell of vodorosli, a clump of seaweed, rank,
scraped from Rialto's steps. Mortality, the tidal musk of sex.
We write in water, mark our passing with an X.

KULDIP **GILL**

Kuldip Gill teaches creative writing at the University of the Fraser Valley (UFV). Author of the award-winning book, *Dharma Rasa* (Nightwood Editions, 1999) and of limited edition chapbooks, her poetry appears in *Event, Prism International, Contemporary Verse 2, BC Studies,* and *The Literary Review of Canada* amongst other journals. Her work has been anthologized, most recently in *Contemporary Voices of the Eastern World: An Anthology of Poems,* (W.W. Norton and Co., 2008). Online, her translations appear at *Poetry in Translation* on the UBC webpage for Educational Insights. Kuldip Gill received a D.Litt. (Hon. 2005) from UFV, and was Writer-in-Residence there for 2006.

My poetics are fluid guides to my writing, based in my biography and my learning, present contexts, past work and engagement with the work of other poets. The fluidity is an outcome of the recognition that my poetics are always emergent, transformative and changing. The central elements are words, and ideas about their sacredness which come from my Indian background; and ideas about the place of poetry and importantly of poets themselves, through the millennia in south Asia.

Ideas about the Indian goddess Vac (word, later the Latin vox and later still the English word "voice"), and about the place of language and its meanings intrigue me. In the Indian tradition, explained by a famous grammarian, the word is eternal and the ultimate reality. Both the elements of form/word/speech, and of meaning, are crucial for any literary effect. In the first element, I include sound (qualities drawn from syntax and syllabic effects) or the musicality of my poetry; and in the second, patterns (structure), imagery (imagination: concrete and abstract imagery), and the context, as important to the unity of a piece, to its whole or "story."

All of these lend themselves to the experience one has of a poem, to what I have referred to in previously published work as its rasa (from Indian literary theory). The outstanding elements I have mentioned above are the rasa of a work and can be explained as the "juice," or the very best parts. These ideas from an ancient literary theory, combined with my knowledge of western poetics, inform my work and keep me intrigued with the endless possibilities of poetry.

Earl Muldoe - Pendant '76

Then, it probably lay in some building
Along the highway, that intersection

We called K'san, a gas station, a few places
With totems of carved cedar, out front.

Perhaps it sat on a rough counter before a window
Where the sun glinted in—caught the gold inverted

"u's" or the salmon trout eye, your finest cross hatching
Still roughly carved, two ovoids, one almost

A circle The hole is round, engraved initials
E.P. M'76 and KSAN – 18k. on the back. The raven

Carrying the moon in his beak, wings outstretched
And you made this small circle—perhaps an ear.

A hole right near his jawbone. Was it
Really like this? You carved it, when?

When the sun dipped into the horizon
And you sat alone beside a transparent light bulb

In the morning after a night on the town? Were
You proud of it as you burnished in the last

Rubbings, the design laid in forever? I've worn it
Around my neck for years, tucking it into my bra

When it didn't suit what I was wearing,
rather than leave it in my hotel room where

It might be stolen. Who did you think would wear it?
Some princess? You never dreamt a Sikh princess?

KIM **GOLDBERG**

Kim Goldberg's latest book, *Ride Backwards on Dragon* (Leaf Press), was a 2008 finalist for the Gerald Lampert Memorial Award for poetry. Her poems have appeared in *The Dalhousie Review, Rampike, Filling Station, Prism International, Front, Tesseracts* and other literary magazines and anthologies in North America and abroad. She co-hosts an Urban Poetry Café on a Nanaimo radio station, creates "poem galleries" in vacant storefront windows, and is a frequent performer at Wordstorm-Nanaimo and other spoken word events on Vancouver Island. In a former life, she was an investigative journalist and nonfiction author.

I am interested in exploring boundaries of all sorts. Much of my investigation takes place under my Pig Squash Press imprint where I build book objects from tarpaper, tin cans, slabs of fir bark. When I house a text about the people I encounter in the underpass within an object made from roofing felt, flooring paper and steel wire, where does the poem end and the book object begin? Where does the book object end and reality begin? The tattered cover stinks of tar and has sharp bits of wire that can snag skin. If I paint the words of a poem on cardboard placards and photograph the placards around town, then glue sidewalk litter to the photographs of those same sidewalks, where does the poem/art end and reality/truth begin? Or are we immersed in one giant PoemArtReality all the time, so vast that we can only recognize it through these localized recreations we call "poetry" and "art"? I live in downtown Nanaimo where I spend a lot of time every day just wandering around with my camera. As I document this landscape of deterioration and boundaries known as Nanaimo's "Red Zone," to what extent am I also probing my own interior Red Zone? Where does the political end and the personal begin? Or are outer landscape and inner landscape just two sides of the same skin? Prose poems are obvious boundary-walker terrain. Do literary genres actually exist? Or is genre merely an arbitrary and self-limiting construct we cling to so as to prop up hierarchy and forestall our surrender to the unknown? By abiding by rules, by colouring/writing within the lines, do we in fact foreclose on the unfettered creative act? Does commitment to "genre" stem from a mentality of fear?

Seed

I was out sowing the seeds of revolution in the clarity
of February's heatless sun when I saw her yarding
on a pipe wrench, trying to pop the head off a
parking meter. Her straw-blonde hair bobbed each time
she jerked the iron bar. I could hear her grunts from thirty
feet away—me and my fistful of pamphlets flogging
existential aphorisms for self-liberation from the Herd Mind.
My entire revolutionary enterprise was invisible
in her hunger-struck fever on this Sunday afternoon
along this empty gut of sidewalk in Nanaimo's battered
core—the so-called "Red Zone"
from which drug dealers are banned (even though
most of them are addicts, and this is where the needle
exchange and homeless shelter and soup kitchen
are located). The private police force hired by
downtown storekeepers was nowhere in sight on this
particular side street. When I could see the grease stain
on her nylon jacket, she woke from her Zen practice, shoved
the wrench inside her coat and retreated to a door stoop,
moulding herself into a faceless heap of thrift-store rags, hidden
in plain sight. Just more anonymous
curbside detritus. As I passed, I wanted to apologize
for intruding, for interrupting her survival, for being so pathetic
as to think I could change anything by peppering
the streets with Sartre, Camus, Thoreau, neatly parsed into
bite-size portions for close-cropped minds. Confronted
by such compression of life, I saw my puny grasp
held no sufficient offering. I glanced but did not gawk
as I passed this primal lump, this uncarved block
of wood, this dark that hoods the light, this nothingness
that will take flight as ten thousand things,
this seed.

GARRY **GOTTFRIEDSON**

Garry Gottfriedson lives in Kamloops, BC. He grew up in a ranching/ rodeo family and still raises quarter horses. Gottfriedson is from the Secwepemc Nation (Shuswap). He holds a Masters Degree in Education from Simon Fraser University. Gottfriedson was awarded the Gerald Red Elk Creative Writing Scholarship by the Naropa Institute in Boulder, Colorado where he studied under Allen Ginsberg, Anne Waldman, Marianne Faithful and others. He is a presenter of creative writing workshops and lectures. He has read across North America, Asia and Europe. His work has been anthologized and published nationally and internationally. Currently, he has published five books.

I bank on my cultural knowledge to write poetry. My poetry covers a broad spectrum of observations both from my First Nations background and from my experience living in colonial Canada. My writer's voice can be harsh and politically charged, revealing the reality and the experience of the First Nations political atmosphere, yet at other times it reflects a more gentle tone — an expression of my love for the land in which I grew up in. In addition, my work captures living memory. It serves as a historical witness to the issues experienced by my people, and it illustrates the present conditions of the living experience within First Nations communities. Considering the nature of my work, my publications are also playful, symbolic and engaging. I am never bored with the use of language. It is playful. It can be compared to photography, when used in the right combination, for it can print a picture in the audience's mind, and that language is fire. Poetry in general is too strong to let die, because as long as there is human conscience then there also exists the will to speak, read and write. This is what cultural knowledge is all about.

The Cross for Mary Magdalene & Me

Mary Magdalene never looked so good,
a skin of lilies
a mouth of thorns
a soul reprieved

she lived at the bottom of the cross,
a head crashing memory
a prayer worthy of love
a heart of spikes

She begged for guidance and forgiveness
as she handed me the hammer
and there was God crying blood
for the both of us

SUSAN ANDREWS **GRACE**

Susan Andrews Grace lives in Nelson, British Columbia where she teaches creative writing and also maintains a visual art practice. Her latest books of poetry are *Love & Tribal Baseball* published by BuschekBooks (Ottawa, ON) in 2007 and *Flesh, A Naked Dress* published by Hagios Press (SK) in 2006. *Ferry Woman's History of the World* (Coteau Books, 1998) won the Saskatchewan Book of the Year Award and was shortlisted for three other Saskatchewan literary awards. Other books published are *Water is the First World* (Coteau Books, 1991) and *Wearing My Father*, a chapbook, (Underwhich Editions, 1990).

It should come as no surprise that a woman who excelled at mathematics and philosophy in fourth century Alexandria would be murdered by monks because she was single, old, beautiful, and had political influence. In recent history Luce Irigaray writes that the thing still most refused a woman is the study of philosophy. All we know of Hypatia's work is that she was inventor of an astrolabe for determining the altitudes of planets and stars and most likely an elucidator of Euclid's Geometry. Yet she merited a murder we remember more.

In *Hypatia's Wake* I continue with my favourite compositional strategy of the serial poem. A serial form, I think, is an expression of the flesh of being: the particular layering of individual existence. The serial form builds a structure of truths and contradictions, beauty and ugliness, longing and loss that are existential realities. If the serial poem was cloth, its weave structure would be peculiar to the person who wears/writes that experience, and recognizable to others who also wear it. *Hypatia's Wake* is a wake made for daughters and their children and to liberate dead mothers.

Hypatia and most women in her wake in history have lived with what Nicole Brossard has very eloquently written about, the double bind. In *Hypatia's Wake* I mirror and examine that bind. These poems are offerings, food delivered to a funeral barge afloat in the feminine imaginary and celebrate Hypatia, philosopher.

Hypatia's Wake

excerpt one

> *Philosophy is the one thing they will not allow a woman to do — says Luce Irigaray.*
> *My friend Jacqueline tells me that drinking gin while reading Irigaray helps.*

Knot   ## Untangle

In a Khamaseen wind
particles just a little larger
than wave lengths of light
scatter red, to cause a blue sun more
rare than the blue moon
but as Egyptian.

           Blue is the colour of my true love's eyes
           and I scatter red.
           Philosophy is not allowed
           but read on anyway, eyes
           skyward, to see the astrolabe soul
           pour eyes's cones into a future
           you cannot see.

Massive building and ancient sea
history's constancy: conquerors
and conquered; humanity and
scholarship.

           The sea is an older victim—
           she sparkles whether poisoned
           or not, reflects the sun
           a famous lighthouse
           at her edge.

Silken knots are the worst—
untwisted floss becomes tangled
by breath.

To spin silk, hands must
be smooth as rose petals
so rub with lemon juice.
Depending upon available humidity
sesame milk may be used as hand lotion
or silk fibres may be soaked in it.

Bombys mori caterpillars
after thirty days of eating
mulberry leaves: a silk worm

rotates two hundred thousand times
      in three days
      not dizzy
but weaves a silky cocoon
out of his spinneret—
      a hole in his head—
fibre the length of
      twelve football fields.

Orestes visits Hypatia
sorts thoughts like rose petals
his command weighty
her freedom a star in Alexandria's
fifth century sky.

The giant god Serapis in 391 AD
already destroyed by a monk's axe on the jaw
his blue skin composed of gold, silver, lead, tin and ground
sapphire, hematite, emerald and topaz. They struck
Serapis and the earth did not open.
The library ransacked by monks
or burnt by Caesar's fire arrows
shelves cleared.

SHIRLEY **GRAHAM**

For three decades, Shirley Graham has written poetry and prose and published her work in various literary magazines. (m)Öthêr Tøñgué Preš published her chapbook *Blue Notes* in 2005. Black Moss Press published her poetry book entitled *What Someone Wanted* in 2007. She works as a psychologist and lives on Salt Spring Island with her husband Peter Levitt and son Tai.

When I was young, the word "poetry" held magic. It evoked the deliciousness of being read to, word-music, the royalty of language and an intensity of emotional connection. It meant a profound "being with," comparable to gazing fully into eyes (people's or animals'), entering thoroughly into play with a child, or absorbing oneself in deeply focused activity. Poetry became a home, a place where I could safely be myself without anyone minding. It remains so, a coming home, whether I read or write it. As a reader, I have found poetry in the works of many favourite poets, of course, but also consistently among short short prose writers like Kafka, Robert Walser, Wolfgang Borchert, Kawabata, Galeano. As a writer or a reader, I know I am home when I remain with the words, following them down their emotional plumb-line until I reach an end, from which, looking back, I feel the inevitability of the piece, that its emotional integrity is dependent on it having exactly the form and content it has.

Italo Calvino, in his book *Six Memos for the Next Millennium,* retold the story of Chuang-tzu, who, when asked by the Emperor to draw a crab, said, "I'll need five years, a country house, and twelve servants." The Emperor gave him all he asked for, and at the end of five years, Chuang-tzu asked for and was given five more years. At the end of ten years, he picked up a paintbrush and with one flourish painted the most perfect crab anyone had ever seen. This is the magic, the inevitability, the intensity I seek.

Blue Three

I. Blue Horse

The blue horse runs in the mist of old Japan, in a painting that hangs on the living room wall of Monet's garden home at Giverny. The sight of him, so full, round, so thoroughly horse, is as heart-stopping as the famous gardens. Brush stroke steed, head down and frisky in thick fog, he perpetually cavorts in the inky mountains of Northern Japan, and in your memory, ever since you saw him, held your breath to his high kicking, vowed to remember the painter's name to look up once home, remembered and forgot the name twice over. Like a lost love, you have scoured art books in stores, libraries, in the homes of acquaintances to see him again, but the blue horse escapes you. With a snort into wet mountain air, he turns, gallops, and is gone.

II. Blue Ladder

You cannot see the top, yet you must start climbing. Above, you glimpse another climber reaching out sideways with one hand as if to touch a passing bird. You wonder what the ladder leans against, what could be that tall. The wooden rungs under your grip are smooth and cool, almost metallic in their feel. After the first several steps, you gather rhythm and begin to enjoy the climb. The air is salty. You imagine yourself climbing a crow's nest to look out over a blue horizon, heading for some unknown land. Slowly, as you tire of climbing, you realize you really are heading for the unknown and you must keep going. Another climber has started below you. This is how it will be. The blue ladder is longer than a life.

III. Blue Crane

Blue feet, blue legs, blue fog rolling over a marsh like slow wind, then a blue line which becomes a beak, a bird's head, a crane standing on the shore of a pond, all the while blue fog and small sounds. In its inch by inch drift to the pond's centre, understand that the crane is all there is. The picture must be kept safely within its frame. A white crane, feet disappearing into green water, head dipping in and out of thick blue fog. Nothing but this. And then, perhaps, just fog. Absent yourself, hardly breathe. A crane in a marsh under fog. Only this.

CATHERINE **GREENWOOD**

Catherine Greenwood's poetry has been widely published in Canadian literary journals and has also appeared in anthologies such as *Long Journey: Contemporary Northwest Poets, and The Echoing Years: An Anthology of Contemporary Poetry and Translation from Canada and Ireland.* Her first book *The Pearl King and Other Poems* was a 2005 Kiriyama Prize Notable Book, and her poems have received a number of awards, including the Bliss Carmen Award and the National Magazine Gold Award. A long-time Victoria resident, she and her husband Steve Noyes recently spent a year in China, where she taught writing and literature at Qingdao University.

Sometimes my poems germinate from middle of the night thoughts after all the busy-ness subsides and things start to float up to the surface, murky protean entities that demand some sort of attention and hint at containing some form or material shape. Usually, though, I have some idea in mind of what I want to write about, and the unbidden images that bug me until I jot them down end up wrapped around that subject, often greatly altering my original intent.

My style and form varies quite a bit – I used to tend toward narrative but lately have been experimenting with metaphor as a means to its own end, larding on the imagery until the poem is jangling under the weight of its own excess. I've also been exploring tensions between physical and metaphysical realms, and those ideas are showing up in some of my poems in a rather deliberate manner. I may change directions soon, and see what happens if I'm a little less controlling.

I like working in pseudo-forms, finding the shape of each piece as I work. Poetry can be play, putting a puzzle together when engaging with structures or certain patterns of imagery. Once in a great while you are blessed with a moment in writing where you hit the right note and you know it (it feels a bit like finding your true pure voice while singing in the kitchen late at night with no one around to hear you). For me, a lot of the time, however, writing poetry is quite hard work.

Black-Tail Deer

Silvery wraiths blurred by snow, rising
on legs slender as twigs. In a fallen forest

deer detach themselves from charred trunks
and listen. Their ears, black-tinged brooms,

sweep the singed air. Smudged muzzles
glisten where they have sipped pure

thought from the streams, that chill clarity
the mind dips into then shivers off

like a drop of ink flicked from
a calligrapher's brush. Twirling blunt

tails, they fade among somnolent birch,
disappear into the edge where pines hide

snow-blind heads in the bristled sky.
Sharp hooves puncture a drift's skin

with tracks, each empty black dot
aligned with the bright illusion

winter has embroidered on the speckled
pelt of the fawn, each transitory knot

stitching up a white story the mule deer
smuggle deeper into the season's

dormant soul. Within every silent bearer
its narcotic cold, the coming melt.

HEATHER **HALEY**

Poet, author, musician and media artist Heather Haley has been published in numerous journals and described as a "Canadian national treasure." She is the author of the forthcoming *Window Seat* and *Sideways* from Anvil Press, described as "brawny and uncompromising" and "supple and unusual." Haley was an editor and writer for the LA Weekly and publisher of Rattler and the Edgewise Cafe, one of Canada's first electronic magazines. She is the producer and director of videopoems, *Dying For The Pleasure* and *Purple Lipstick*, an official selection at over a dozen international film festivals. RPW Records released her critically acclaimed AURAL Heather CD of spoken word songs, *Princess Nut*, in May 2008.

One thing I am is a poet. I will write poetry though I'm not particularly concerned with form or media, and I will write poetry whether others deem it relevant or not. I cannot abide didacticism. Neither do I pull any punches. I believe that in this world, being an artist is a political statement.

Whore In The Eddy makes the political personal. My narrator imagines stumbling upon a slain woman's body. *There but for the grace of God go I.* The woman happens to be a prostitute. She lies down next to her so they may gaze at the stars together.

When I was a girl on a New York City sojourn, the only job I could find was in vice, tending bar at the Baby Doll, a topless joint near Wall Street. Thus the place was frequented largely by bankers and CEOs. In possession of an unconscious dread of men, I was disgusted watching the suits ogle heroin-addled dancers on the tiny stage. I too was bribed, pressured to take my clothes off, and tempted, for I too was desperate and in need of cash. I know abuse. I know the prostitute, the stripper, the drug addict. The people I depict are not carnival freaks that I stare at fixedly in shock and amazement; they are part of my experience.

Whore In The Eddy

Gazes up at ballooning clouds as if imagining
frogs. Giraffes. Corvettes and barns.
As if Neptune's head has heard
her pleas. Sent me. She looks like a mannequin.
As if by law of nature, a stripped woman's body
looks like a mannequin after it floats
to the surface in a rainforest denuded
by steam donkeys and timber sales. All matter
from the depths is netted by log jams.

She stares at me. Cannot see
the pebbles embedded in my knees.
Or my face, not so sweet.
No bubbles, just the stillness
of standing water. No trace DNA.
No hard earned cash. Only cool airstreams
of aspen leaves. My grasping
hand takes hers, skin gliding onto my fingers
like a glove. A device. We share features
any porno-masticating, regular working stiff
joe wants in his garage
between the red pickup and the Crestliner.

We watch the rim of night, a spiral arm
of stars, their slow light two million
years too late. Naked eyes decipher
Orion the hunter. Cassiopeia. Bright knots
of the Double Cluster. Mars appears.
I look the other way, to the North Star.

GENINE **HANNS**

Genine Hanns is an acrylic artist, poet and fiction writer from Victoria, BC. She graduated from the UVic in 2005 where she completed a Double Major in Writing and English and plans on taking an MA in Writing. She has published poetry in *Canadian Author & Bookman, Cross-Canada Writer's Quarterly, Dandelion, Descant, Ice River, Late Knocking, and Northern Light*. She has also published articles and poetry on websites in Canada, the United States and Great Britain. She currently has a manuscript entitled *The Language of Water* with Ekstasis Editions in Victoria. She is in the process of publishing her first fiction novel, *Dancing with Snakes*, co-written with Alan Mettrick.

If art imitates life, then poetry is the most honest representation of living. The love of language, the power and value of the spoken and written word, is our only deep and lasting source of communication with each other. I love bringing chaos into order through the therapeutic beauty of writing poetry. Making sense of events that happen in my world, documenting them as important, relevant and even timeless, presenting my own unique voice and vision with a strong emotive quality to capture a particular situation or event that readers could identify with themselves; something that resonates within, offers them joy and comfort on a primal level, and connects us together in order to support, validate and understand our vulnerable human experiences. This is what compels me to write poetry and what I desire to achieve in my work.

More Than an Abortion Poem

When I had dialled the wrong number
of days in my blue dispenser of estrogen,
progesterone, a little spirit, small as a poppy
seed, entered my earth womb,
sprung from her dream
of opium. My nights were stolen
from me, my days swollen
with fear, kicking against my ribcage,
the tick tock hiccups, my anxiety riding
roller coaster hell. And then, she slowly
began to devour me, rearranging my flesh
into tidy pillows, carving my breasts
into honey hives, my bladder, a Hoover
dam, my spine a continental shelf,
floating in amniotic waters,
while I, a stranger, heavily laden
as a suitcase, travelled
through the foreign port of my own body.

I told myself, I am not ready for this.
Yet my mind, wool gathering, needled up
each thread of guilt, knitted fantasies
of a face, a name, a child pushing
on a swing, up through the never-ending
sky, joyful fingers curled around a kitten,
stroking her ears, a string of giggles,
and eyes, innocent as Eve's and delicate as
bone china, the pale blue of unspeakable
sorrow saying, "Let me in. Let me in."

How can I tell her
like some quack spiritualist? "You must
understand. It is not like killing.
For I have heard the soul
does not enter the body
till the seventh month. And I have even heard

the soul enters the body with the first
breath. It is not like killing."

And she will say to me: "Then have me
and give me up."

Give her up and wonder all my life
about her eyes, her face, her voice…
are they like mine, or his, or both of ours?
Give her up and my remaining days
will find her lodged inside me like a silver hook,
pulling me back to her nightly
as I dream the untouchable softness
of her skin, the sweet grass smell of her,
the name I would have given her
echoing in the long chambers of my ears
as I am hauled unhappily
through my life like baggage,
for eventually I would have to see and know.
I cannot give her up.

If this little spirit could know or understand
the soul never dies, and if she cannot learn
her life's lessons with me, then it
will be with someone else. If I could satisfy her
that this is true, and myself also,
then perhaps I could begin this bloody plan
I contemplate on moon drenched nights
if there are no stars to condemn me
and no sky to remind me, up there
she waits for me.

DIANA **HAYES**

Diana Hayes came to Salt Spring Island in 1981 to finish a book of poems and never left. She completed her BA (UVic) and MFA (UBC) in Creative Writing. Her published books include *Moving Inland, The Classical Torso in 1980* and *The Choreography of Desire.* Recent travels have taken her to the Greek Orthodox monasteries in Thessaly, the Aran Islands of Ireland, and the oyamel forests of Michoacan, Mexico where she studied the monarch butterfly. Her upcoming pilgrimage will take her to the Casa de Dom Inacio in Brazil. She considers poetry an essential food, as is her amante, Mario. www.dianahayes.ca

Poetry has been an essential food since childhood, when my grandmother recited from the sonnets of William Shakespeare and encouraged me to listen to my own inner voice. I was fortunate to live in an extended family where grandparents had the time and leisure to explore with us the world of nature and the imagination. I wrote my first poem at age twelve: a passionate plea to stop the world's destruction from the point of view of a rock. I often skipped classes and escaped to the books of Ezra Pound and W.B. Yeats. Poetry was a feast that never left me hungry. It was a way of life, a blood connection.

The power of the spoken word was instilled early on, and during my university studies I attended many memorable poetry readings. I will always remember the voice of Robin Blaser reading from "The Moth Poem," the stage sparsely but dramatically set with a large brass gong which he sounded at the end of the reading.

Poems connect us. They are ambassadors when grief blinds us, when joy takes our breath away, when memories visit in the night and don't leave a name. Poems are rhythms of peace in a world of ancient battles. They offer refuge from the front lines when there is little to believe or trust. They offer a map to the heart, a path otherwise lost in the helter-skelter of our too-busy minds, a flute to follow when the dissonance of our weary lot rings in our ears. And finally, poems are followed by silence, the space between words, the knowing that cannot be told with language.

Where Have You Gone?

Whatever our age, whatever we know
Or don't know about the invisible workings of this earthly life
We ask, again and again, where have you gone?

For Diane, August 3, 2005

Always Pucinni filling your house as you prepared feasts for friends
Brewed Torrefazione while Floria Tosca's despair danced across the lake

You were clear as a star on a bright night when you were near water
I still see you canoeing St. Mary's, waiting for the fish to bite

Saga's mahogany polished like crystal, mirrors, labyrinth of dreams
As you cruised the Inside Passage, summers never ending

Giving twilight a glimpse of your passion as your mind worked prisms
Colours and light forming the true brilliance of your smile

Elegant silks and linen, boots of Italian suede tempting the nurses' wardrobes
As you always found time to feed patients, asking after their day

I too was lucky to know you as we juggled politics and personalities
Health boards and hard noses, guarded what was most at risk

The autumn I left for Europe you gave me your blessings
Told the lions in suits to take notice, listened to the stories in my poems

What I celebrate now is your vision for open spaces, breaking the heart's barriers
What I want most is to know you are traveling down the long river

Without burdens or losses, without the memory of a body's failings
And the siege of cancer raining its cardinal cells all over your beauty

And where are you now, if not with translucent angels and Giacomo, singing
E non ho amato mai tanto la vita! And never before have I loved life so much

IAIN **HIGGINS**

Iain Higgins was born in Vancouver and has lived most of his life on the West Coast. His poems have appeared in numerous small magazines and in *The New Canon: An Anthology of Canadian Poetry* (2005). His first collection of poems, *Then Again*, appeared in 2005 from Oolichan Books. His translations of contemporary Polish poetry have been published in magazines in Canada, the UK, Ireland, and the United States, including *Descant, London Magazine, Metre,* and *Chicago Review*. His translation of Adam Czerniawski's *The Invention of Poetry*, was published in 2005 by Salt. He teaches Medieval Studies at the University of Victoria.

The medieval Scottish word for poet was *makar*, or maker, which is of course exactly what the word poet means in its Greek etymon. In this view, which I share, a poet is fabricator, and a poet's making is variously a remaking, a making up, a making do with, a making away with, even a making out — since often the desire to make the sort of wordthing we call a poem is prompted by desires as deep and complex as any erotic longing. A poet fabricates a poem by weaving into a single new fabric strands from other tissues of matter and meaning that we call the world, language, and the imagination. Hung before an attentive eye, these fabrications at their best can change how we see: they both block our access to the world and restore it. But poetry is not only a matter of matter refabricated, of tapestries that reveal wordworlds and whose mediating words thus reveal the world yet again. It is also a form of song abstracted from its directly musical origins, and so it don't mean a thing if it ain't got that swing (as Irving Mills put it for the Duke to sing) that comes from its roots in the lungs and the heart. Sound and the movement, the play, of sound are part of its sense, embodying it — which means that a *makar* in making is kin to frogs and birds and even alleycats. We are in our animal as well as our human element when we make poems.

Avatar

Christ, yes, who here amongst us now cannot still
   recall the hour when we first heard those electric mouths
crackling like songbirds from the advanceman's chariot?
   Haste ye! Hear ye! Step right up & lookie lookie!
   Himself—yes, yes, Himself—is here, is here already!
Our hands fell from our work like shot hens and never
   returned to such airy pursuits, no, but sprawled useless
as liverspots in our chastened laps, lively only
   when Himself demanded our once-calloused applause
or his clothes be ironed. Oh, but the chariot was grand.
   Its high sides shone in the sodium halflight like tin
teeth in a movie pirate's grin, and we were so taken
   with the glow we hardly noticed the mismatched wheels,
their spokes repaired with leather and faux duct tape,
   the axle made of lignum vitae from Eden, last of its kind
since the place was gutted for the blowout yard sale.
   Himself followed in his fine foreign rattletrap,
a motorcar he said, pronouncing it *motorcade,*
   parting the thin crowd—we were a family more
than a village even—like a conjuror's Red Sea
   or a thicket of gnats gashed by an annoyed hand.
Himself was driving, as always, head cocked just so,
   to be seen in profile from his exemplary side,
all three hundred and sixty degrees of it, he said,
   smiling a smile decisive as a glasscutter's stroke,
a lit rod wedged between his yellowed fingertips
   where it would dwindle and rise again and again
like his contempt, his fury, and his secret gadget.
   Not that the dead hand that grasped the wheel, that scribbled
autograph after autograph when free from fondling,
   was thick and hairy-knuckled. No, no, the flesh was
tender-firm, human, the man's nails neat as new moons.
   As if a god he was, prince of the self-denying,
self-deceiving, self-indulgers, a true maestro
   of music, dancing, and the mind's finer matters,
with which he graced our former home, ignoring
   our fly-pocked cobwebs, our swarm of tawdry offspring,

and the poverty of our worldly unvoided heads.
    He hung his hat on the corner of the plasma screen,
switched off the mike, disdaining the mere magnificence
    of amplification for his own basso profundo,
and took the privileged chair outside our circle—
    for that was his real distinction, to sit apart and
yet retain the centre as his own domain. From there
    he spoke in sermons, poems, lectures, manifestos,
while the children pricked quickly at their wax tablets
    on which truth was misunderstood as everlasting
words and errors were made: *works like a charm for do no harm.*
    And yes he was a real charmer. Worlds flowed in spate
from his mannequin mouth and swirled into being
    like the finest concretions of nectar and teflon,
invincible, as if to prove the rightness of the slogan
    above the bull-necked eagle on his ring: amor meum
omnia vincit—my love does it all. He spoke
    his love in a language of consonants like fishbones
in a slit throat, the tongue in broken teeth, but
    so subtly it might have been an aria resonant
with vowels and sung by angels before the betrayal.
    He's so like just so incarnational, the young ones said,
and we had to agree. Himself was the real thing,
    what we call a copper nickel in our now-dying tongue.

ALAN **HILL**

Alan Hill lives in Burnaby, BC and has been writing since 2001. He started writing while working for two years in Botswana. He originates from the west of England in the next village to his big influence, the poet Charles Tomlinson. Alan is the proud grandson of one of the Britain's leading trade unionists of the nineteen fifties and is married with a baby daughter. He comes from a typically culturally diverse West Coast family of Welsh, English, Vietnamese, Finish, Aboriginal and Scottish ancestry and has had poetry published in a number of small English periodicals and by Poetry Scotland.

I am not, in any traditional way, a religious man. Like many millions of human beings I don't believe there is an interventionist god that has my personal interests at heart. Likewise I don't believe that science and rationality, in themselves, carry the great answers to life's mysteries that they promise. If you try to rationalise and pull apart a beautiful object, in the end you are left with broken pieces and the object you started with has gone. Poetry is a way of re-connecting with mystery and otherness, while not leaning too much in either the rationalist or traditionally religious direction. It is a tool that borrows from both the spiritual and the rational, pulls them together in ways that allows exploration of feeling, history and place to a depth that can't be reached any other way.

Visiting Malcolm Lowry
– Vancouver 1953

An unwilling Christ that has been
slashed with an axe by the pinheaded
pioneers of a provincial certainty.

His face is glowing like a night raid
on Dresden, lit by the incendiaries of
sorcerers and demons, tax payers,
letter writers and the non human eye.

He is squatting on a sanity that has
broken his legs, bricked him deep
in foliage and ocean at the back end
of the British Empire, under a sun
that has lost the nerve to set.

Here are the remains of a man,
fenced in frontier space, in his
driftwood Consulate for the lost:
He is heir to an impossible brief
that has been scripted by devils.

A drinker with a writing problem
being shamed in front of a packed
jury of unfinished manuscripts:

Every day is the day of the dead
for this mess of a man, lipless and
slivered under a myopic thickness
of cheap glass, scavenging
for scraps on the lip of a crater.

ROBERT **HILLES**

Robert Hilles lives on Salt Spring Island with his partner Pearl Luke. He won the Governor General's Award for Poetry for *Cantos From A Small Room*. In the same year, his first novel, *Raising of Voices*, won the Writers Guild of Alberta George Bugnet Award for best novel. He has published thirteen books of poetry and five books of prose. His second novel, *A Gradual Ruin*, was published by Doubleday Canada in 2004 and now is in paperback. His books have also been shortlisted for the Milton Acorn People's Poetry Prize, The W.O. Mitchell/City of Calgary Prize, the Stephan Stephansson Award, and the Howard O'Hagan Award. His latest book of poetry is *Slow Ascent.*

Poetry for me is rooted in the human. As far out into the cosmos as we may travel there is no escaping the raw, important truths of earth and body. I am all for abstract concepts in poetry as much as I am for exploring emotion and the complexities of the heart, but to pretend that emotions do not exist is to work with only half of the poetic equation. Because of this, I feel that there can be no complete separation of ideas from their emotional counterpart. Often, we are detached from certain concepts, even abstracted from them, until we feel them. Death is a good example of that and so is love. It is only when we mourn the loss of a loved one or experience our first breakup that we finally sense the full complexity behind these much used words. Yes language, place, craft, invention, excitement and even story all make poetry the most enduring of the written arts but without a human pulse it does not age well. Precision in language is as important to me as form. I think one of the great poems of the twentieth century is "Church Going" by Philip Larkin. In that poem Larkin does not waste a single word and each image is as current and vital as when he wrote it more than 50 years ago. Much of that poem focuses on the metaphysical and yet it is Larkin's presence in the church, what he feels as he takes off his hat, and what he comes to by the end of the poem, that make it great. What I value most in poetry is that shaping of human imperfections into something greater than human, not quite divine, but as close as we get.

A Long Row of Days

– Chekhov –

Take one brown piece of paper
Fold it in half from the right
Take another and
Fold it from the left.
Lay them side by side
Leaving a gap between them
Look into that gap
Tap your fingers on the desk
Turn to one side or the other and listen
That sound just now
Out in the yard
A thrush or crow
It doesn't matter
That is the sound of you
Entering that gap
Filling it with all of your being
That is you
Going away for good.

Someone who enters the room later
Will find an empty desk
No paper, no gap
No sign of you
Just the flat rosewood surface
Polished without a scratch
Beautiful really in the way
Only wood can be beautiful
That will matter to them.

KAREN **HOFMANN**

Karen Hofmann grew up and lives in the southern interior of BC. She completed an MA in English at the University of Victoria, and teaches English and creative writing at Thompson Rivers University in Kamloops, BC. She has published poetry and fiction in many magazines, and placed third in *ARC* magazine's poem of the year contest in 2005. In 2007, she won the Okanagan Short Fiction Contest. Her first collection of poems, *Water Strider*, was published by Frontenac House in April 2008.

My poems use image and language to chart the processes of subjectivity, of perception, memory and reflection. I am interested in tensions, surfaces and duality, and in using these aspects of experience and of observation of the natural world to create a map of the boundaries between experience and perception. In my poems, the landscape and the natural world are extensions of the consciousness, in which perception may both float freely and be reflected. Tensions in the landscape and in language provide metaphor for the gaps or strains in consciousness, for the effort to achieve and maintain consciousness.

Highway 97 North

A canvas belt flung north,
belt stripped through its loops,
flung out across a rumpled bed,
flung, not quite flaccid,
over folds, plateaux.

a machine belt suddenly
snapped, rearing back,
small tragedies in its wake.

Along the highway the discarded past: stripped slopes, remains
of snow. Rust of pine. Breadcrumbs
of brown bottles, tossed glitter
of homemade CDs.

The Cariboo trail, the gold trail. And today's traffic:
a few SUVs, businessmen, the Coca-Cola truck,
hawk hunched for the crossing accident.
The short haul.

To live here is to live in and out of time:
the long drives filled with perpetual forest,
with devices to suspend life, to skip ahead,
to blur passages,

the walks measured by fenceposts, the hour's trudge
that takes in the badgers' empty set, copse
of broken aspen, moose-grazed,
boom of pent ice. The raven's seventeen
voices of boredom. Coyote's strobe-light
glance.

The landscape strung out between
absence and the next event,
perpetually too old or too young.
Violence the only connect.

Your hair whiter each trip
you make into town. Scars
shimmering threads. One day, I say,
I'll drive the road to its end.

SEAN **HORLOR**

Sean Horlor grew up in Victoria, British Columbia, and currently resides in Vancouver. His first poetry collection, *Made Beautiful by Use*, was published by Signature Editions in 2007. Described as a "a striking and, yes, beautiful set of musings on belief, sex, and power," the collection garnered a number of positive reviews across Canada. His work also appeared in the groundbreaking *Seminal: The Anthology of Canada's Gay Male Poets* (Arsenal Pulp Press, 2007). He is currently completing a collection of fashion poetry with Toronto poet and playwright David Brock.

I've challenged myself as an author to write poetry that doesn't romanticize the natural world, which is something many Canadian writers do very well. Consumer culture, large urban cities and the way politics shape our lives interest me more than meandering through a bramble patch. I am also not a fan of overtly confessional writing and have difficulty writing personal poems from a first-person viewpoint. The poetry of an unfinished thought and the poetry of the half-spoken sentence fascinate me, as does poetry where the implication of what isn't said becomes more important than what is. My writing begins and ends with a focus on finely crafted images and strength of voice. In a recent bookninja.com article with poet and novelist Aislinn Hunter, we debated the return of formalism in Canadian poetry and whether or not that is another thing that is making contemporary poetry contemporary. My stance in this arena hasn't changed. I still believe that the resurgence of form doesn't sociologically fit the Canadian psyche. Formal constraints don't match our social restraints, which are few. Although I respect writers who are subverting form and transforming it into something new and different, I believe that the poets who are claiming that formal concerns alone make Canadian poetry better or that formal concerns somehow put our authors on a level playing field with American poets are wrong. I expect pop culture and the retelling of shared cultural stories and fables to continue to inform my writing in the years to come.

Fixer-Uppers

They all said there's something you should know
about me they all asked why
haven't I met someone like you
before they all said yes they all said please
come back stay over I don't want you to
go it's not too late they opened
windows standing they offered chairs at tables in restaurants
in cars at the end of roads in theatres on boats on trains
they slept on the right then the left then the right
again they all said I think I'm in
you are my best you are my first I have never I am better
you'll see without you I could never
one asked will you marry all asked
do you love me when can I see you why aren't you
returning my they all brought beer some brought condoms
some brought other rings they all apologized no one
brought the right question the right way at the right time
all were angry they all hit in their
own way some harder when it counted harder
kiss me harder they kissed they all did they all
asked what do you want do you need do you
believe in God you don't believe me why
do you always how can you ever do you mind if I hate
when you tell me what this is what are we will you be
can we have we what have we done I think we
should I know we will can I try you just don't why
don't you ever turn out the switch on the cut the close the don't
slam the open the hang the flush the brush the wash this can you
pick me could you call a order us a few I don't know when
I'll be back do you love him love her more than
I will kill you if you you're wrong I won't ever
will you be can we be what have I done I think
we should I know we will can you just
they all asked will it hurt how can I trust
I don't do that I won't do that next time you
ask me first or don't bother coming back.

JODY **JANKOLA**

Jody Jankola graduated from Concordia University in 1996, with a BA in Creative Writing and English. She has been residing in Powell River since 1997, raising her daughter, Skeena. She is a member of the Malaspina Writers' Association, and was the editor for *River City Runes*, a compilation of writings by members of the group. She has taught scriptwriting, playwriting, poetry and short fiction workshops and has had her poetry published in *The Wayward Coast*. Jody is currently working as a technical writer to pay the bills, and writing poetry to remain alive.

I was born into poetry. I was raised on the stuff. My mother was a poet. Was, because now she is a painter. She switched professions in her mid-fifties. When I was growing up she would lock herself in her bedroom/studio every afternoon and write; a big "Do Not Disturb" sign hung on her door. I was both jealous and proud of her poetic passion. I missed her when her poetry took her away to readings and cross country tours, never mind her daily regime. But I was oh so eager to tell all my friends that my mother was a poet. I showed them all her books and bragged away any chance I got. She and her friends were akin to Rock Stars in my eyes. It was the 60s and the 70s. It was very hip to be an artist. It is no surprise that I wanted to follow in her footsteps. In grade 5, I won a national poetry contest. The prize was to be published in a book called *Pandora's Box*, along with other winning kids all across Canada. My poem was about a beautiful yet distant woman. My mother, undoubtedly. Later, in university, I was drawn more to the short story form. But eventually poetry crept back into my work. I love to play with images. "Show, don't tell,"— a phrase forever etched into my writing psyche from school. I want to paint with words. As I get older, there is less to say and so much more to see. "A photo says a thousand words." Words that paint the image that touches another soul, reaffirming, yet again, that I am not alone. And in the end the poetry that took my mother away now keeps me company.

Heron Is God

Waiting for the school bus this morning,
we saw the heron again,
flying overhead,
landing in the yard behind.

We could not see where he perched,
but he was talking to Skeena,
telling her that she and I were going to have a happy life.
She could interpret this, she told me,
from the rhythm in which he was squawking.

A grey winter day on Donkersely Beach,
before Skeena was born seven years ago.
My husband and I were debating whether Christ was God.
He was a new Christian,
I, a doubter.
Right in front of us, a heron suddenly rose up and took flight
"Heron is God," I said,
all the while knowing my husband wouldn't respond then,
but that I hadn't heard the last of this blasphemy.
I didn't expect him to write a song about it,
especially not a love song, about me.

The heron has been appearing ever since.
After my husband took his life,
the heron appeared for my lover while he was missing,
lost in the war he had been fighting in for more than the three years
I had known him,
battling the same deadly opponent my husband had,
and lost.
The heron flew into a tree across the street from my porch
and perched there until I knew in my heart my lover was going to live,
he was going to be alright.

And then again last week,
arriving too early for my tutoring job,
Skeena and I drove around the block and there was heron,

taking flight in front of the car.
One squawk and he was gone.
Skeena didn't know how to speak heron then, so there were no interpretations,
but once inside my students home-stay,
the young Korean boy presented an essay on heron's cousin crane,
complete with two origami birds made as part of his project -
one for Skeena, one for me.

His essay said that in Korea
they believe the crane is a symbol of peace, joy, happiness, and love.
They believe if you make a thousand cranes and give them to your lover,
your lover must love you forever.
I hung my one crane over my bed.
I am not sure what Skeena did with hers.
The next day my lover phoned to say his final good byes.
My services no longer needed.

I don't know how to make origami cranes,
nor do I have the inclination to learn.
But today heron flew overhead,
and Skeena told me he said that she and I were going to live a happy life.

The heron has never lied to me before.

ELENA E. **JOHNSON**

Elena E. Johnson was born in New Brunswick and has lived in Montreal, Toronto, rural Uruguay, the boreal forest and her little yellow tent. She now makes Vancouver her home. An MFA student at UBC, she has worked as a park naturalist, ecology researcher and community arts facilitator. In the summer of 2008 she was writer-in-residence for the Kluane Alpine Research Project.

Much of my writing is based on my field experiences and travels as an environmental educator and ecology researcher – work that has taken me to many wilderness areas and urban centres in Canada and abroad. Nature, adventure and the idea of home (or belonging) are ongoing central themes in my poetry. I am currently at work on a series of poems that draw from wilderness navigation techniques and ecosystem theory in order to explore the fragmented yet intrinsic relationship between human beings and the natural world. Navigation serves as both tool and trope: a lens through which to contrast the urban and wilderness environments, and a metaphor for our greater struggle to find our way through the complexities of the modern world.

where we are from

the swedish-speaking edge of finland.
russia. norway. each time i ask my father

where are we from? he adds a new
country to the list. salt-fish

journey. voyage by ship. change
of name. from these we string

stories with our new
language, never heard

by our great-great-grandparents.
i inherit, instead of

words: sudden feelings, images. this heavy
clasp. i have no cloak. i inherit

quick flight from danger, ability
to love, appreciation of flame. i

inherit the sea, the longing
to swim. i inherit this moment,

culmination of all the knives
and fire and singing footsteps.

i sit at a table in a warm kitchen
in a winter city. sunlight

spills through the window. it
calls me

to walk outside
in the snow before dark.

SEAN **JOHNSTON**

Sean Johnston is originally from Saskatchewan and worked for many years as a surveyor. His latest book is *All This Town Remembers* (Gaspereau, 2006). *A Day Does Not Go By* (Nightwood, 2002) won the 2003 ReLit Award for short fiction. He lives in Kelowna where he teaches literature and creative writing at Okanagan College

This poem is a small scene that touches on universal big themes: life and death. In my poetry I try to make the private public in as quiet a way as possible. I try to write about the private search for meaning that is always in danger of becoming shabby in the light of its articulation. My poetry has the same relationship to autobiography as my fiction, which is simply that I am human, and so is the speaker; I try not to rely on the authority of details from my specific experience. The logistics don't matter. The search does.

Green Lawn, Under the Trees, a Cemetery Across the Street

Sitting on the stoop with a cigarette, calling the dog and shaking keys
in my holey pocket, I wait for a sign

she is making her way back—a smile
from this city's strangers, a quick bark, the momentary speed of her shadow

behind the fence, before she runs through the gate. Behind me, my children
marry, because we're moving in a week

and while packing I found a black suit
for a four-year-old boy, a six-year-old's white dress. Their solemn rehearsals

mythologize their past—they pretend to be their mother and their father.
I have heard them talking. I don't know where

they learned their lessons. No sign
of the dog; I will have to gather the children and walk. Their mother is across

the street lying in a one-year-old hole, and I don't want to walk, this tiny bride
on one side, her still-learning groom

on the other. They will say the dog
is lying on the lawn above their mom. She won't be. But we'll wait, and see.

EVE **JOSEPH**

Eve Joseph was born in 1953 and grew up in North Vancouver. She worked on freighters as a young woman and traveled widely before moving to Vancouver Island where she now lives in Brentwood Bay. Her work has been published in a wide number of Canadian and American journals and anthologies. Her book *The Startled Heart* was nominated for the Dorothy Livesay Award in the 2005 BC Book Awards. She has an MA in Counselling Psychology.

Poetry is smarter than I am; it knows things before I do and pays attention where I am oblivious. It notes the incidental and receives the uninvited; it listens the way we did as kids with our ears to the rails before the train appeared.

When I was very young, poetry was inseparable from imagination. When it rained, I saw fairies huddled under toadstools and walnut halves, flipped on their backs, sailing out to sea; at night the sky was a sea where fishermen cast out their gold and silver nets to catch the herring stars and dormice fell asleep beneath red and blue delphiniums. Poetry invited me into the invisible and the illogical; it didn't matter that I had never seen a delphinium or that I searched but never found a fairy. What mattered was the invitation; the certainty that the world was full of wonder and I was a part of it.

I returned to poetry after a long absence. I can't say it came looking for me. That's too easy. Nor can I say that it resolves anything. It is, more often than not, completely inaccessible. I was going to write that poetry has become a way of living but that is not quite right. It has more to do with being awake, a way of listening: ear pressed to the rails. It is still, after all these years, an invitation into the world.

Questions

I want to ask poetry where it was for all those years. Where was it when I chain-smoked my way through Vancouver bingo parlours and where was it when I traded my Penguin classics for True Crime stories? I want to ask it about waitressing in Chinese restaurants and slinging beer in Indian bars and about hitch-hiking and smoking dope and seeing the prairies for the first time. I want to ask about underground rivers and the homelessness of rain and how it knows what it knows and why it knows so much more than I do. I want to ask poetry where it goes when it disappears and if it was there when I shot pool and crashed in cheap hotels in small towns across the country. I want to ask it why it drew me close and then let go and if it led me to the dying as a way to keep me alive. I want to know how it found me on a red bench in a mountain cemetery and how it slept beside my daughter in a graveyard full of lost boys. I want to ask if it appeared one day as an albatross weaving across our wake and if it showed up another time as a young girl dancing alone at night on a seawall in Riomaggiore. Did it travel with me like the tip of a blind man's cane as I stumbled into my life? I want to know about blindness. I want to ask poetry where the birds went when they disappeared and how it was they reappeared in cursive loops like a new language above the daffodil fields one afternoon in late March.

DONNA **KANE**

Donna Kane's work has appeared in journals, magazines and anthologies across Canada. She is the author of two books of poetry, *Somewhere, A Fire* (2004), and *Erratic* (2007), both published by Hagios Press. In addition to her writing, Donna organizes readings, retreats, festivals and writer-in-residence programs throughout northern BC. In 2007 she worked with the city of Dawson Creek in naming a street after singer/songwriter Roy Forbes, and in 2008 she will be organizing the third Muskwa-Kechika Artist Exploration Camp. Donna is currently completing a degree at UVic.

Having lived in northern BC all my life, my writing is definitely influenced by place. It is also influenced by an enduring obsession with human perception. What can we be certain of? I'm drawn to poetry in which metaphor and plain statements of thought or belief are balanced in a way that invites the reader to consider their truth rather than take them as given. When this balance works, it seems we are given a whiff of the ineffable, an adrenaline rush of the best sort. How a poem accomplishes this is a mystery to me, but I daresay that rush and mystery are intertwined and key to what keeps me reading, and to what keeps me writing.

Idiot's Song II

But talk to me talk to me
or die soon before I do
I'll come where your body is
tho it answers me nothing
            —*Al Purdy* (Idiot's Song)

No miracle how the sun in its proximity
to the earth would not, at any other distance
have been just right, would have had us die
with less anguish than we do now
our curves of flesh spectacular
and finite. No miracle,
except as it relates to cherry trees,
to spiraled shells pressed, cosmologically speaking,
against an ear, we
a variation on a theme.
But talk to me

            talk to me
as light falls on the hawthorn leaves,
the purple columbines.
Your voice rising above each mathematical mystery,
no mystery except I don't get it, the precise
add and subtract of cells loaded with baggage.
If I feel I'm being watched,
no doubt it's me watching me,
a paranoid reflexivity,
a gaze that won't unglue or die soon
before I do.

Our cells could tell stories
that would burn your socks off —
nuclear furnaces, the iron-sink-spew of fierce
and fast. What chance do we have in any of this?
A lemon slice floats in my glass,
and I'm happy.
If that's not enough then this:

I'll come where your body is
when the night is clear and the only thing
that staves off panic is knowing
you're a freak of stardust too.
We'll address the countless starving planets,
the sun that in our gaze of devotion
blinds us for our troubles, the flat lining universe,
its steady slide toward dark, dead, and cold
an inspiration to lift our glasses
to this momentary blip, this party going on,
my breath, your voice, its perfect ring
tho it answers me nothing.

MICHAEL **KENYON**

Michael Kenyon is the author of nine books, most recently *The Biggest Animals,* a novel (Thistledown Press, 2006), and *The Sutler,* poems (Brick Books, 2005). A new collection of poems and a novel will be published in 2009: respectively, *The Last House* (Brick) and *The Beautiful Children* (Thistledown). His work has been shortlisted for the Commonwealth Writers Prize, the SmithBooks/Books in Canada First Novel Award, the Baxter Hathaway Prize in fiction, *The Malahat Review Novella Prize, Prism international's* fiction contest, the Journey Prize, the National Magazine Award and the Western Magazine Award. Two stories took prizes at *Prism's* fiction contest. He divides his time between Pender Island and Vancouver, having in both places a private therapeutic practice.

I've been writing for forty years. In the past it involved the production of a maze parallel to what we call reality to offset overwhelming experience. I needed it to be automatic, indirect and accidental, so I could get at deep processes. I wanted to escape difficult life, especially in the social sphere, and eventually I wanted to reach others for whom the act of reading was, as it has been for me, indulgent, illicit and liberating.

I've been experimenting with form, adapting obsessive forms and inventing my own. Counting and rhyming are so compelling to me now that I will readily sacrifice meaning (what I mean) for shape and music (what I might mean if I was wise).

I love the physical world and want to get it down in words. I'm delighted and moved by haiku and other forms that pay attention to the visible, here and now. But near the core of my being is the desire to track the dreaming above and below the worded landscape. Surrealism and Dadaism, sure, but that's just the beginning. As I get older, I'm more in touch with a voice I lost when I abandoned my accent on emigration from England, age fourteen. I wrote my first poem at fifteen, in Canada, so the poems are a trail of crumbs I'm following back. Shakespeare is more and more familiar.

Courtyard
for Denise

A day of dogs when they stop the bombs.
Then leaflets, quiet. Birds outside
the window in the hedge. We know when
it's time to go, to put on frailty

like a disguise until it mimics
the thin branching of time, the burn
of autumn before colours die and
days lie still, the same old door open

each midnight to Mum and Dad fighting,
their fight not ours. Autumn's yellow
was not ours, nor were the blood-red leaves,
and starlight fades as the day strengthens,

starlight that lit the river that
led us here and meanders toward
a future distance we measure now,
especially now, in every cell.

Nor was Christmas ours, and not houses
(though gardens were lovely), nor cars,
holidays, countryside, the sea, and
all those times we loved and were loved back,

the moment we made a child out of
almost nothing, what you came with
and I gave away, a child we don't
know yet. We wait by shuttered cafés.

We wait with pigeons (who know to wait
patient as stars who wait for night).
We wait in the warm courtyard and scan
the wild stone hills above the crop line.

SCOTT **LAWRANCE**

Born in 1947 and raised on the coast of British Columbia, I began writing when Kitsilano was a state of consciousness as well as the home of Jackson's Meats, took part in BC's fledgling Peace Movement, the introduction of Tibetan Buddhism to this land, and the genesis of Raincoast Chronicles. I retired from one of the best school districts in the country several years ago to begin the "real work," poetry, meditation instruction and wilderness vision fasts. I am the clinical supervisor for CanAdventure Education. I am a father and grandfather and live on Cortes Island with Dianne.

First, a few questions: do the requirements and desires of poetry remain the same or do they change, in response to conditions, personal, cultural, political or otherwise? What do "the times" demand? Is Leonard Cohen's "what is the revolution asking from me?" still relevant, or even more relevant? Should poetry have a moral function at all? What is the relationship between civilization as we know it, during this state of seeming collapse (or at least reorganization), and poems; the function of repressive tolerance, consumerism and commodification of art (poetry) and artists (poets)? What about identity, as a person and as a "poet," after post-Modernism?

And because there are no easy answers to these questions, the poems arise in response. I try to get out of the way as much as possible. Certainly and at the very least, I attempt to allow room for the unknown, the miraculous, the awesome. I wish I could say that for me, poetry becomes a way of unmasking. If that were so, each poem would reveal something hitherto unknown, concealed or unsuspected. I am suspicious of any attempt to write a poem "about" something. I am deeply suspicious of the teaching of poetry. The models lie near at hand, proliferate even. Poems are born of the intercourse of previous poems, and the good ones squall mightily, drenched in fecund afterbirth.

But perhaps, poetry might best be understood as practice. As in sitting, and other forms of meditation, it is not that "practice makes perfect." Rather, these are ways of bringing forth, of showing or revealing, how things actually are. Ah, this is how we are, nothing more, nothing less, nothing added, just how it is, in this moment. What Kerouac pointed to with "spontaneous verse," and Chogyam Trungpa with "first thought, best thought."

Interrogation

i.

I have no information about that
I have no information about terror
I have no information about Guantanamo
I have no information about Abu Ghraib
I have no information about Palestine
I have no information about Israel
I have no information about Congo Rwanda Sudan

This is the barking of a wild dog
This is the snarl of a tooth in the fog
This is the smoke of epidemics in the red trees
This is the needle of hope in the cedars dripping

I have no information about that
I have no information about ghosts family dynamics or turntables
I have no information about the Mayan calendar

These are screams of a man under duress
A man captured by history
Whose controls are losing their grip
This is the ship sending out its signals
Bring beer we're going down.
O save save save save
Who unleash this hooded eye

ii.

I have no
information about the horror
I have no information about the suffering
I won't tell you about any of it

Alien intestines I have no information about
& I also won't tell you about my skull

I have no information about the fat hands
That have been placed around the planet's neck
So please don't ask

I know nothing about it
I know nothing about the perverse theatres
Of leash and naked pyramids
& knowing nothing I can tell you
nothing hooded
I know nothing about metal folding chairs
I know nothing about Nicola Tesla or electricity
I know nothing about bamboo nothing about water
Don't ask I won't tell you cyanide

Hatchet men in suits come next
Wearing garments of paper
Papyrus contracts
I've never seen any papers
That isn't my signature
& I'll deny it if you ask
It isn't anyone I know.

CHRISTOPHER **LEVENSON**

Christopher Levenson, born in London, England, emigrated to Canada in 1968 where he taught English and Creative Writing at Carleton University, Ottawa, before moving to Vancouver in August 2007. He has published eleven books of his own poetry, most recently *Local Time* (Stone Flower Press, Ottawa, 2006) co-founded and edited *Arc* magazine, founded the Arc Reading Series and co-founded the Harbinger imprint, specifically for first books of poetry, of the now defunct Carleton University Press, and edited three poetry anthologies. He has traveled widely in Europe and Asia and has developed a keen interest in South Asian literature in English.

After adolescence, when I saw virtue in obscurity and cherished "being a poet" rather than writing poems, poetry has been for me above all exploration, a way of discovering what it was I felt or thought or saw and then, using as many as possible of the resources of language, attempting to communicate this with sufficient accuracy of suggestion and resonance that it would mean something to other people. Although hardly ever lyrical in the traditional sense, my poetry is very concerned with sound values such as assonance, and internal rhyme, and with cadence and verse movement. Partly as a result of four years in the '60s at the Iowa Writers Workshop, my work has become more informal and colloquial. At the same time, encouraged by the examples of four of my favourite poets, Marvell, Yeats, Lowell and Larkin, I have tried to interweave my social with my personal concerns.

Ode To CDG
(Charles de Gaulle Airport, Paris)

Even more than music, or muzak, an airport
is international, the ultimate
gated community and, if no longer
elite, at least self-sufficient.

With its intersecting spars and high-
tech brushed steel, this is no-one's home:
here we are all transients, leafing through magazines,
sprawling on well-designed benches

to catch a few minutes sleep. It does not work.
Though heart and eye might otherwise rejoice at
clean lines of boutiques, elegant walkways,
PA warnings, boarding announcement
remind us not to relax. At all hours we know
we are being scanned by hidden cameras,
everything's taken care of, we are protected from contact
with every element except fear, and have nowhere to go.

TIM **LANDER**

Tim Lander was born the day Hitler marched into Austria. Evacuated from London to the North Country during the years of the war. He was sent to an English boarding school at the age of 6 till he was 18. Called up in the British army he served in Malaya. Studied Geology and Zoology at London University and immersed himself in T.S. Eliot. He arrived in Canada in 1964, lived and worked in Vancouver with Intermedia in the 70s, went to UBC, obtained a BA in Edmonton. Married and divorced he has 5 children. He moved to Nanaimo in 1977. He has published over 50 chapbooks of poetry as well as 6 books of poetry. His most recent is *Inappropriate Behavior* (Broken Jaw Press, 2006).

I've been scribbling for 50 years and I no longer think I am the world's greatest poet but hope to keep scribbling and producing chapbooks till the day I die. "Chap" in chapbooks comes from the Anglo Saxon "Ceop"– cheap, swap. Poetry that poets can afford to buy or exchange. I believe poets should publish their own work. I believe in the Culture of Poetry and that hierarchy is anathema to culture. Poetry is the most basic and most deeply felt language art. Both the most private and the most public. It makes more demands on the audience than any other art form, for in reading a poem, the reader must go more than halfway to meet the poet. Reading poetry is itself a severe discipline so the poet in clarity, and the tricks of rhetoric must go halfway to meet the reader. The ancient Norse god of Poetry was Brag, poets are all braggarts.

How Do You Write A Poem ?

In times of war
 how can you write a poem
  that will express the suffering
   and the pity
    and the love of God?

How can you write a poem
 While God and his angels sleep
and the politicians
 think they have an answer
but do not even understand
 the question?

God is Great
 maybe
but God is hidden behind
 the processes of History
and now we watch entranced
 as empires decay
  and grind themselves
   to dust

But the pity of wars
 as armies seize
  the hospitals
and the women and children
 pack up and flee
and carry away with them
 in their hearts
  such sorrowing
such anger
 such bitterness
What poem can encompass this?

But how can you write a poem
  denying all the millions of Africa
   and the refugee camps?

women
  with their tiny scraps
   of borrowed land
their children gathered around them
  waiting patiently for food to come
  from the agencies
their children dying around them
   driven from their meagre farms

How can we write a poem
  to bear witness to all this
so far away
  yet daily in our
   living rooms?

In what kind of language
  can you express the grinding of history
that grinds down the multitudes
  like a woman grinding corn
   in a stone quearn
a daily labour
  for the sustenance
   of her skinny family?

What metaphors express
  the camps in the desert
   the bad water
    dystentery and death
     the fading light
      in a child's eyes?

What poetry is adequate
  for humanity as brought to us
   daily
    by the CBC?
watching horrors

squeezed between the commericals
 while we sit chewing
  on cheese and crackers
   on the couch in the living room

while beyond the bright screen
 of our TV sets
  reality is happening
   right now
    in our living rooms
     and far away

How do you write
 a poem
  for the times?
for the future
 and the past?
for the children
 and the grandmothers
for the grandfathers
 and the great salt sea
for the tight knots
 of history
and the sorrowful Earth?
How do you write
 that poem?
how do you set those words
 upon the page?
how discover those words
 in what dark dictionaries?
what waste tears
 can coin these metaphors?
what rhetoric
 what cadence
  what form
   what rhyme scheme
can we use
 to write the final stanzas
  of the history of the human race

and the planet
  that will bear evidence
  of our masterful technology
    rolling through space
      eternally
with its burden
of memory?

PETER **LEVITT**

In addition to poetry, Peter Levitt has published journalism, essays, fiction and translations from Chinese, Japanese and Spanish. The poet Robert Creeley has written that Peter Levitt's poetry "sounds the honor of our common dance." Author of twelve books, he received the prestigious Lannan Foundation Award in Poetry. His most recent book is *Within Within*, published by Black Moss Press. Other books include *Bright Root, Dark Root; One Hundred Butterflies; Fingerpainting on the Moon*; and *A Flock of Fools: Ancient Buddhist Tales of Wisdom and Laughter*, co-authored by Kazuaki Tanahashi. He lives on Salt Spring Island with his family.

Inasmuch as I can locate a singular poetics, I'd have to say that mine are variable, found only in the act of composition as each poem shapes itself in the making. I have no a priori conditions, constraints or guidelines other than to do my best to ride the horse I'm on, love the one I'm with, as the song goes, in the mutual and intimate act by which a poem and I come to life, emerge, develop and move toward full expression. Jackson Pollock's "when I am in my painting" comes to mind. For me, articulation depends upon the quality of silence I sometimes manage to maintain. It is here, where there is nothing to hear and no way to hear it, that my poems begin to speak. Primarily, then, poetry becomes an act of listening and presence. To fully articulate what, in the moment of living, must be said, in a way that also carries that silence as an undiminished fact of the poem, has been a lifelong attempt and true affair of the heart. I try to hold that silence as a source of being, even as it holds me, so that my poems accomplish what might be called an energy transfer from source, through poem, to reader, without much loss of the original energy found at the source itself. On the rare occasion when this is accomplished, I experience an act of recognition where I see and understand again (re cognition = to think or understand again) what I had not recognized before. A seeming paradox. Yet, if the poem is made with the original energy more or less intact (from any of the countless sources living provides), sometimes a reader experiences an act of recognition as well.

The Unremembered

There is no way to put it back together,
there is nothing to put, no back,
and together is a close approximation,
a flash of what only seemed.
The weave and colour of the cloth,
the seam pressed into the leg,
a sleeve with its opening hole
are glimpses of paradise or desire,
tastes of summer water or the first
of lips with that brown skinned girl
I heard someone say was *mine*.
No one can hold that still, and I
stand somehow shamed yet amazed
at how quickly it flies now I see it,
each day more and less than before.
It is not a melancholy that so catches
my breath almost before I can exhale,
there is no bitter taste of living. To hold
what we can as precious, to feel with
our hands, our skin, what can't be held
is the dream of living, the extent of now.

The past goes as it must,
a distraction, a bent truth
we once believed though to know
what's slipped behind us like a scene
with red canoe and two girls for the moment
singing helps focus on what remains
in a life to do. This is my preoccupation
as lips dry, memory departs,
the place I learn to attend,
though slowly as ever with faults
unremediated and known. I
count each moment by the name
of my wife, my children, a grandson.
They've become the watch on my wrist,
the reason I ask for time. And the earth,

whose wind and water and dust
gives more truly than any other
what can be held, if briefly;
a kingdom for a horse, foolish man,
is nothing compared to that.

To locate where I am in this local
world I listen for the evening rain
as I undress for sleep. I admit
I am disappointed when it doesn't come.
Then I walk to the window and look
once across the dark meadow
toward the lake beyond, and upward
just in case, still with a child's delight.
Each step forward or back takes me
to where I lie down, each deliberate
breath freely released.

RHONA **MCADAM**

Rhona McAdam returned to Victoria in 2002 after living in England for 13 years, and spent 2007 in Italy studying food culture at Slow Food's University of Gastronomic Sciences in Parma. Her fifth and most recent poetry collection is *Cartography*, published by Oolichan in 2006.

My writing roots were nourished in the supportive and lively prairie poetry scene of 1980s Edmonton, where I studied with Douglas Barbour and Bert Almon and witnessed the birth of the Writers Guild of Alberta. Following that, during the dozen or so years I spent in the UK, I immersed myself in the poetry world of London. It was a time of rare privilege, as I was lucky enough to encounter poets and poetry from every part of the English-speaking world, and beyond. As a result, I returned to this country with a much different personal canon than anyone else I encountered. My ongoing links with prairie poets and poetry through the Saskatchewan Writers Guild have enriched my time in Canada, and my writing, even as I strive to maintain some literary links with Europe, through visits and workshops there.

Lost

Sometimes when the car paused
my father would point to a shop
or a gas station and say
that was one of the places
she'd phoned him from, lost
in her own town, and he'd have to find
and pilot her home.

How many such occasions were there,
I wonder, losing myself
the reference points he'd guarded
those final years, in which he was
for the last time able
to do something essential.

Four years now since he followed her
to ground. Spring again in this city
they returned to again and again
from trips abroad, where she followed him
down the streets of his youth; to the town
where her father was born; to my home
in its cage of one-way streets
that baffled even taxis.

My first years back here
I was always getting lost.
My father's directions grew more vague
as street names faded
and we drove in widening circles
looking for landmarks.

The day she died in a renovated hospital
we spent twenty minutes
traversing the old parking lot, looking
in vain for the new entrance.
When we finally found her,
tethered to machines, her face a mask,

no one had words. We sought out the cafeteria,
unmarked and distant, directions hard to come by.
Sat with our plastic wrapped sandwiches
and paper cups of water, trying
to imagine how we'd got here.

SUSAN **MCCASLIN**

Susan McCaslin is a poet and educator, the author of eleven volumes of poetry, including her most recent, *Lifting the Stone* (Seraphim Editions, 2007). She has edited two anthologies on sacred poetry, *A Matter of Spirit* and *Poetry and Spiritual Practice*, is on the editorial board of *Event: the Douglas College Review*, and is a poetry editor for *The Journal of Feminist Studies in Religion*. Susan lives in Fort Langley, British Columbia with her husband, and has a daughter in university. She is currently working on a new poetry cycle called *Demeter Goes Skydiving*.

Poetry is a dialogue with silence where language steps lightly but is voluptuously committed to the dance. Since my earliest jottings, the words that arrive have been ravished by something I have called variously, "Spirit," "God," "the divine," and "holy oneness." Since conceptualizations fail, all I can say is that the spiritual life for me is more like falling in love than embracing any kind of belief system. The mystics William Blake, Teresa of Avila and Julian of Norwich have become not just muses and mentors, but luminous companions. Yet the fascination remains with how language can snuggle up to the unspeakable, die, and burst out again like some new species of exotic bloom. Mysticism is to me the heart of religion because it, like poetry, is experiential. In recent years, my orientation has become much more eclectic and interfaith, though I am happy to be grounded in a contemplative meditation practice.

I have edited two anthologies that ponder how contemplation and poetry are related. Some of my cycles focus on specific mystics like Blake and Teresa. In "Letters to William Blake," the speaker fires off a series of epistles to Blake. I can also remember the first jolt on hearing Teresa's feisty voice, knowing it as distinct from my own.

I have been a college instructor of English for almost thirty years, teaching courses like "Biblical and Classical Backgrounds." For most of that time, the writing of poetry fit nicely into the margins of my teaching life. Now, having retired, or as some say, "re-fired," life affords me the opportunity to place poetry at the very centre. Today I wait for poems, tend poems, and let go of poems. In the end, being in the creative flow is what makes the present, present.

Demeter Ascends Mount Norman
On Pender Island, British Columbia

She could have been dropped by helicopter,
but prefers to hike over potholes,

up switchbacks to the summit,
only 800 feet, but the highest peak on the island.

In the Mysteries,
a mystic comes with eyes closed,

and, later, mouth agape,
but here,

with islands stretched like whales' backs,
the slate sky pearlized,

to shut the eyes would be irreverent
for the eye wants to linger along the strait,

pick out cormorants, wharves, ferries.
The eye is on vacation here,

back in the image-flow.

Islands sleep in earth's ear canal,
and Demeter, gazing, is mothered

in the Mother at last,
stepping up to the tectonic plates,

penless
before the great utterance.

GEORGE **MCWHIRTER**

George McWhirter, born in Belfast 1939, came to British Columbia with his wife, Angela, in 1966. Apart from his stays in Mexico, he has lived there ever since and for the past thirty years in Point Grey, Vancouver. He has two Canadian children, Grania and Liam, and three Canadian granddaughters. His most recent poetry books are *The Incorrection* (Oolichan Books, 2007) and *The Anachronicles* (Ronsdale Press, 2008). His version of Euripides' *Hecuba* was produced by the BlackbirdTheatre Company at the Vancouver East Cultural Centre from late December 2007 to early January 2008. On March 13, 2007, he was inaugurated as Vancouver's first Poet Laureate.

Being no hunter with a gun, I want instead to shoot things (that elusive animal, mineral, vegetable quality in them) into life on a page with the animus of the verb, and vice versa, to shoot the elusive nature of the verb through with the animal, vegetable, mineral animus of things, to find the argument, the drama in the grammar, parts of speech, phrase, to pursue the sentience in the sentence, and in the process, with work and prayer, make sense out of the senses.

The rector's warden at Holy Trinity Anglican Church on 12th & Hemlock is named Nova Leaf

The storm scribbling in the trees, the dirty sky
Much pondered, much laundered through the mind, the road,

Twisting, wrings itself out of rain on a journey to dry socks,
The snare of warm feet.

According to the hotels, all the highways and airways
Lead to these and a bed in Calgary, as we journey East

From Vancouver, and not to Calvary with Jesus

Close by Jerusalem.
The wind spins over the ears with the izz

Of a barber's razor set on No.1, the closest cut of all.
No palms, this far from Galilee, dead leaves

And branches garland the asphalt,
While over the hills, the Chinook moves

As softly as the eastern exhaust of the Pacific.

Whose hands, but those of Jesus—
No Canadian's can span us

West to East.

Here, says the Great Desert Resort
From Kelowna to Albuquerque,

We wait on you. We too were once
Wet and tempestuous young souls

Waiting for our mother to finish
The tormented laundry

Of the sea.

JEAN **MALLINSON**

Born in Vancouver, Jean Mallinson spent her childhood in the Similkameen Valley. She attended UBC, The University of Toronto and Simon Fraser University. She has published a book of short stories, *I Will Bring You Berries*, a book of poems, *Between Cup & Lip*, and a brief memoir, *Terra Infirma: A Life Unbalanced*. She is one of the five poets who wrote *Quintet: Themes and Variations* and she has published essays in *Geist, Vocabula Review* and other periodicals. She now lives in West Vancouver.

Poems provided a place of enchantment and refuge when I was a child. Their dactyls and anapests took me elsewhere. When I read later that the gods in the Rig Veda clothed themselves in meters to escape death I thought I understood why.

A hymn I love asks "How can the creature cry 'Praise'? How can the creature cry 'Save?'" Writing a poem is an attempt to find an answer to these questions. Everything is a gift; the world, language, time, the conventions of prosody, the body, the self are all given. A poem is an attempt to give back, an offering.

There is an eros of poetry rooted in the love of a subject, the desire to embody it, and in love of language. Milosz says "a poet is in love with the world." Auden says "In poetry you must love the words, the images and rhythms with all your capacity to love anything at all." A poem is, as Wallace Stevens says, "the cry of its occasion" and also, as Auden says, formal and ritualistic. It is both expressive and conventional, both a mask and a revelation. Its formality and its expressiveness are entwined.

A poem is, William Stafford says, "a collaboration between an attentive self and language." It calls out, "Listen to what I have to tell you." Elegiac because what it refers to is gone, past, it is hopeful in its gesture toward a possible future in which the poem will be read. It is resuscitation – mouth to mouth and mind to mind – the poet's words in her mouth and mind to her words in another mouth and mind, summoning up the occasion the poem celebrates or the loss it laments.

Tinnitus

Penance for all my privacies, my inward-looking –
this thin metallic veil
between me and the world's messages.
Reliable trill, I can count on you
like an aching grudge or a depression:
you are always, after the hubbub,
still there: obstinate cricket,
perched on the rim
of my left ear's labyrinth.

You are attrition,
the piercing wind that will wear away
the arabesques of my ear:
invisible bird's whistle
against the whorled bone.

Listen, I'll ignore you, obscure you
with music, with voices,
but when the world stops speaking
you pipe up and shrill
that you have been waiting, my faithful,
for this rendezvous,
droning your monotone
on the edge of my imagined mind.

I remember Beethoven, aureoled bust, icon
on my childhood copies of Etude
slanting on the upright piano:
his mind, where he composed hymns
to the gods who attended him there,
became a cacophonous junkyard
where sounds pitched and clanged
like unballasted objects
in a ship at sea. So, tempest-tossed,
he loured and scowled, but still contrived
melodious cadenzas
above his private clamour.

Little tin whistle, you are my secret cross,
my hidden torment,
in spite of which I smile and smile.
And you have your uses:
through you I can bargain with God
against the major plagues
that might wrack my body,
shatter my mind.

Sometimes you are a reassurance,
almost: you speak to me
of survival: you tell me to count
my blessings: I could be listening
to my heart's drum, a thunderous lob-dup,
to the torrents of blood and lymph
in my body's rivers. But only you
have escaped to tell me:
I'm alive, I'm alive, I'm alive.

VERA **MANUEL**

Vera Manuel is Shuswap-Kootenai from the interior of British Columbia. She is the eldest daughter of the late Grand Chief George Manuel and late spiritual elder and activist Marceline Manuel. She is a writer, poet and playwright. Vera has written and produced plays about cultural oppression and genocide including: *The Strength of Indian Women* and *Every Warrior's Song*. Her poetry and short stories have been presented at venues across Canada and the US and published in journals and anthologies. Currently she is completing a CD of poetry and is the recipient of the 2005 World Poetry Lifetime Achievement Award.

Poetry became my way of telling a story about subjects too painful to talk about within my family, community, tribal groups and nation. Poetry gave me license to say out loud everything that others were afraid to tell. An elder told me once that "poetry is a gentle way of talking about painful things."

For years I used my poetry as a tool to help people to heal and never thought to publish it or to use it for any other purpose. As long as the words that came to me could help to open doors for others to get at their feelings and their own words that is all I cared about.

Both my parents and most people of their generation were residential school survivors. My father also spent a significant portion of his adolescence in a TB hospital. When I was a child no one talked about the past, but I grew up in a home full of silence, shame, violence, incest and rage. The way I survived was to keep silent like everyone else, but I always wrote poetry. When I look back on it now I realize I was not as silent as I thought, between the lines the stories are all there. Poetry helped me to find the words to tell, to connect and to resist my tendency to isolate. In the telling I have gained many allies. Poetry is a powerful source of healing.

My father was an orator who could hold the attention of huge groups of people with his passion and commitment to the land. My mother was a storyteller who passed on knowledge about the Kootenai culture and land. Their gift was their ability to speak from the heart where poetry comes from.

The Catholic Church

My mom used to be vicious at the Catholic Church.
She would call those priests and nuns right down into the ground.
There was a time she would not set foot inside a church.
At funerals she directed her prayers to Napika from the front steps
Peering now and then into the darkness waiting for service to end.

The only time people go to church is when there's death.
They walk 10 miles in the cold just to church when some dies.
When I die don't ever bring me to that place.

I used to hate the church too although I never knew why.
I guess I hated them because I loved my mother.

Every time we passed by that vacant, grey structure
That once was St. Eugene's Indian Residential School
I could feel my mother's anger, brittle and hard,
Exploding beside me, shattering sharp like broken glass.

She never cried like my father, she told it to me straight
And hard-edged, embittered and enraged so I became afraid.

That ugly, grey building was once like prison to me.
That ugly place still standing there,
All our cheap DIA housed falling down
But that place still stands reminding us
Someone ought to burn it down.

Fearful that she just might do that one-day I'd distract her,
Make her change her mind; say something to make her laugh.
I loved to listen to my mother laugh.
She had a good sense of humour,
An offbeat way of viewing the world
That's what got her by all those tough times.

Ought to burn that place down too,
She'd say as she tossed her head toward the neatly-spired,
Whitewashed Catholic Church that still dominates
The centre of her village today.

DAPHNE **MARLATT**

Daphne Marlatt's long poem in prose fragments, *The Given* (McClelland & Stewart, 2008), reads like a novel and was written as the third in her trilogy beginning with *Ana Historic* and *Taken*. She is currently collaborating with book designer Frances Hunter on "Between Brush Strokes," a limited-edition poem about the life and work of the BC painter/poet Sveva Caetani, due from JackPine Press (Saskatoon) late 2008.

I seem to be currently resistant to poetics statements. Suspicious, perhaps, of the attempt to define what goes on in the impossibly shifting instants of composition. Even that word, composition, suggests putting something together (definitively). But my experience while writing is more of a reaching for something (the poem is after) that is constantly escaping, while discovering other recognitions along the way.

Having abandoned the traditional notion of measure, I suspect that the kind of poem I write becomes a way of taking otherwise a measure of the world I currently, or fleetingly, in a series of attempts at attention, inhabit. Perhaps making a reading would be a better term, as there is always the possibility of alternative readings, whereas taking a measure suggests something much more exact. Language as a medium is highly associative, which can be cause for despair or improvisatory play, depending on one's tuning at the moment. And of course a reading is only ever partial because what's at play is also what hasn't yet found a way of being said/read. Our insistently global world appears very bleak at moments, but play can be transformative, can offer new takes on what felt limited and closed. So I continue working towards a poem as a series of openings.

revising the local
for RKK

     i

dark days out on a limb
'careful now' anxiety
opens the door
for the smallest one

hey-Zeus lurks out there
dawn's catpaw fog
a cover for rainspout
loiterers, alley raccoons

or hungry hands lifting
home-free garbage under
the bald eagle's eye atop
a once-catholic spire

       -- not even the smallest sparrow
       He said, shall fall

when i was a child

     ii

how reconcile God with tsunami
wreckage except by separating
out "the chosen," the "elect"

– belief pitted against belief –

pity the minds behind a
warehouse full of parkas and
stiletto heels –

"where *is* Sumatra?"

who is Thailand?

     iii

sun clearing
grey miasma cold of frosted
grass, the slow dissolve

foothold, paw print
sneaker stamp oblivious
of what we forfeit, this

     intimate self conjunct
   with other intimate selves
   without number

so Kiyooka, bent over a desk
doors away and years ago

wording a different
possible

ROBIN **MATHEWS**

Born in Smithers, BC in 1931, Robin Mathews' early impressions combined the great beauty of the Pacific Coast (where the family took up residence) with enervating Depression poverty. After the Second World War – which he was too young to go to but old enough to benefit from as positive effects were produced in the economy – he gained "higher" education, a university career, a wife, three children, and a life of cultural and political activism. He writes plays, poems, short stories, cultural theory, political criticism and a regular Internet column on Canadian affairs for vivelecanada.ca.

A line of graffiti on a wall not far from the Britannia Public Library in East Vancouver reads: "I write, therefore I am" A good beginning. Not far, perhaps, from the defence by a verbally shy person who said: "How can I know what I mean until I write what I think."

As time passes, writers (people, that is, who write seriously as part of their lives) not only write because they are writers but because they have something to say.

A college student told me a few years ago that there can be no such thing as political poetry. "But," I replied, "poets write of that which moves them passionately. If what we call politics moves a poet passionately he or she will write political poetry — as Lampman, Acorn, Livesay, Fiamengo, F.R. Scott, Neruda, Blake, Milton, Shelley and others have done."

As I do. I write to free human kind from oppression, injustice and suffering. That means I have to write about injustice, political fraud, colonial-mindedness and fawning greed in my own country. I have to write about the depradations of Capitalism and the brutalities of Imperialism. Because the US — and US capitalism — are presently the dominant, brutal, imperialist forces most perverting Canadian democracy, justice, freedom and love of the Good, I must write about US Capitalist Imperialism.

Like all the "political poets" I list above, I write — as well — about many of the other things poets feel passionately and write passionately about.

Exile

They think they have to go away
among alien structures with worn memorials,
down streets paved by foreign hands.
They believe you have to look in shop windows
at books you can never read
while women walk by whose voices
caress the unfamiliar light in a way
you despair of understanding.

In this our own land
our own place is being torn from our hands.
We breathe through broken flesh,
scoop water from our rivers
drained for foreign owners.
The roots of our being are torn up
to make us migrant workers
in our own land,
to make us lost souls
searching for a common language we can use
to organize resistance
to begin the long fight back that ends our loss
this exile.

ROY **MIKI**

Roy Miki is a Vancouver writer, poet and editor whose book, *Surrender* (Mercury, 2001), received the Governor General's Award for poetry in 2002. His latest publications are *Redress: Inside the Japanese Canadian Call for Justice* (Raincoast 2004), a work that explores the Japanese Canadian redress movement through a creative blend of personal reflection, documentary history and critical examination, and *There* (New Star Books, 2006), a book of poems. He received the Order of Canada in 2006.

Poetics Q&A

Reader: I've been asked, as your reader, to have you talk about poetry.

Poet: Aren't you being used? After all, didn't I create you?

R: Maybe so, but once created I am free to ask questions. Why are you so defensive?

P: How would you know?

R: Sorry for pressuring you, but if you're willing to continue, where would you begin?

P: I'd say, if poems were removed from our lives, we would lose a mode of thinking that is crucial for our emotional and intellectual health.

R: If poems are so crucial, why do people seem to have such a hard time with them?

P: Well, poetry comes from language forms that are intricate word constructs.

R: You sound more like a critical theorist than a poet.

P: Relax, you can be both.

R: Oops, my fault. Please continue.

P: Despite appearing peripheral to the big issues of the day, poetry enables us to be conscious of our always on-going interaction with all life forms. Poet Louis Zukofsky once talked about poetry being "precise information on existence out of which it grows."

R: No kidding. Then poetry must be both personal and social.

P: An excellent point, but sadly too often the social dimension is ignored. When poems expose assumptions that numb us to conflicts and injustice, people may shun what they say. It gets even more complicated because, for poems, what is said is enacted in its form.

R: So, if I read you, poems can change us but only as long as we figure out ways of inhabiting its forms.

P: Now you're getting somewhere.

Early Morning in Taipei

All along he thought
he understood until he
stood under the canopy.

Non-synchronous lines
so moist the earth gave
up secrets. The rain-
drops gathered on cars
in the graying dawn.

History's hollow
tunnel again the
slow boat to China.

The shake up in blame
routes (no reason) haunt-
ed him to no end.

I saw the scooter in
the beamed up showroom.

Curvilinear
all so malleable
neural indices
one level of skin

Print bore the datum
of incendiary
tongues of flames casting
the on-lookers (un-
recorded) in shades.

For goodness sake give
the guy a break he
only gathers moss.

The evidence tastes
like ironing filings
or was it filling?

He overheard the
question while he stood
in the virtual
island in the mid-
dle of the causeway.

PETER **MORIN**

Peter Morin is of the Crow clan of the Tahltan Nation of Telegraph Creek, BC. As a practicing writer and artist, Peter's work looks deeply into decolonizing through relationship building and speaking one indigenous language. Peter recently spent time working in Lower Post BC and Watson Lake YT, organizing art projects, writing competitions, bannock making and digital video camps with skate competitions for some totally awesome aboriginal youth. His most recent visual and performance work includes "Team Diversity Bannock, the World's Largest Bannock Attempt," "7 Suits for 7 Days of Colonialism" and "Stop, Drop and Bingo."

For the past seven years, I have been working on developing a writing practice that combines my lived experience as a Tahltan person with my experience of living that worldview within these Western frameworks. My past written works have addressed these ideas as the "Cultural Body." My current artistic focus is around a study of construction technique used in the historic art works of my community, and developing a written practice that incorporates more of these traditional skills as the framework for developing written works. This new research focus has expanded to include aspects of indigenous language (understood as something both spoken and embodied) as a form of knowledge and practice. It is my experience researching this new focus that models of indigenous knowledge practice, and their ways of creating meaning, can grow rich meaning in their reflection back onto the larger systems in which we live.

In my nation there is a story of the light. This story is sometimes referred to as our creation story. For me, the story enables a vision of the respective knowledge and practice of our community identity. The story reminds the listener about the need for searching out knowledge, along with the sharing of that knowledge with the larger community. Like this story, my written works are about illuminating these new ways of knowing in a respectful manner and adding them to the larger story of our community. In my work I am searching out the light and presenting the results of that research to the larger community. My artistic voice is a reflection of the practice of my Tahltan knowledge.

My voice comes from the land, from our traditional territory.

The things I leave behind for Ravens

(Our Raven likes shiny things)

1.

I leave books with Tahltan information written by white men
wrapped in red cloth.

(For our Raven to read)

I leave books with Tahltan information written by Tahltans
wrapped in red cloth.

(For our Raven to check the facts)

I leave books with First Nations politics written by whoever
wrapped in red cloth.

(For our Raven to source)

2.

I leave arguments about leadership
wrapped in red cloth.

(For our Raven to deliberate)

I leave angry emails about who did what to whom
and why I should vote for the other guy
wrapped in red cloth.

(For our Raven to mourn)

I leave the unsure-ness
wrapped in red cloth.

(For our Raven to pray for us)

3.

I leave teachers that correct our English into proper English
wrapped in red cloth.

(For our Raven to rage)

I leave teachers that inform us that We are getting in their way
of labeling and accessing our kids
wrapped in red cloth.

(For our Raven to rage)

I leave councilors and teachers that believe that Ritalin
is the only solutions for our kids
wrapped in red cloth.

(For our Raven to rage)

4.

I leave learning our language to teach to our kids
wrapped in red cloth.

(For our Raven to hear)

I leave trying to learn two languages, and English, to teach our kids
wrapped in red cloth.

(For our Raven to witness)

I leave being accused by the system when trying to teach our kids
wrapped in red cloth.

(For our Raven to carry)

I leave trying to fix up a trailer on the rez for our kids
wrapped in red cloth.

(For our Raven to help)

I leave not getting paid for three months
and being told I was stealing the money from the kids
wrapped in red cloth.

(For our Raven to clean)

I leave watching the two truly weird and brilliant kids argue
even when they should be best friends
wrapped in red cloth.

(For our Raven to remember)

5.

I leave these beads wrapped in the red cloth.

I leave the beads my grandmother used wrapped in the red cloth.

I leave the beads her grandmother used wrapped in the red cloth.

I leave our Tahltan words wrapped in the red cloth

I leave our Tahltan words I remember my grandmother using
wrapped in the red cloth

I leave the Tahltan words my mother spoke to me wrapped in the red cloth.

In honour of our Raven

JANE **MUNRO**

Jane Munro's fourth collection of poetry, *Point No Point,* was published in 2006 by McClelland & Stewart. Her previous books are *Grief Notes & Animal Dreams, The Trees Just Moved into a Season of Other Shapes,* and *Daughters,* a finalist for the Pat Lowther Award. She is the winner of the 2007 Banff Centre Bliss Carmen Poetry Award.

A poem has its own soul. As it comes through me, it takes what it needs to become itself, drawing from my resources of image, of language and of experience. My context informs it — helps it fit into a particular time and place. Perhaps the poem has had many lives, but each time it's different. My notebooks are full of words. Mostly, they're as transient as thoughts in the stream of mind. It's not always easy to recognize a poem when it's still unformed. I get clues. Something takes root and begins to grow. I may feel different physically. I may wake up in the night and have to go and write. I may get a mute hankering for something I can't quite put my finger on. Once in a while, a poem will fall fully formed onto the page. I think a book is itself a poem. Except, I've never had a book "fall bright." Maybe, someday, one will.

I develop a technique for unlocking doors one-handed

Always carrying too much stuff.

Ten months after my father's death,
he has loosened fifty years from his frame.

A doubled spruce. Salt air in blasts. Candles on the table.
Your calls. Your voices. Asters. House wren.

A bird's flight through the banquet hall.
Out the other door. Gust of cold.

What I didn't know was closed begins to open.
A small wind pushes the heart ajar.

Is it this simple? In the lap of a boulder,
a pool of salt water.

Maroon sea star's rough skin.

SUSAN **MUSGRAVE**

Susan Musgrave's novel *Given* will be published by Knopf in 2010. *When the World is Not Our Home: Selected Poems 1985-2000* is forthcoming from Thistledown in 2009. She has been nominated, and has received awards, in five different categories of writing: poetry, fiction, non-fiction, personal essay, children's writing and for her work as an editor. She is an Adjunct Professor with University of British Columbia's Optional- Residency MFA in Creative Writing Program and divides her time, unevenly and uneasily, between her home on Vancouver Island and on Haida Gwaii/Queen Charlotte Islands.

When I first started writing poetry, at 14, I penned Odes to Smokestacks and Factories, peppering my verses with cigarette butts drowned in cold cups of coffee. My father questioned whether my poetry would "survive." He had been raised on Keats and Shelley and admired poetry of higher thoughts, Beauty and Truth.

Yeats wrote about the intriguing contrast between the "deliberate happiness" of Keats's poetry and the sadness that characterized his life. It was the fashion for the Romantic poets to use lofty language to write about lovely things (larks, nightingales, etc.) but today the tendency is to use beautiful language to describe the undesirable and unpleasant situations in our bartered and battered and less than perfectly happy human lives. Beautiful words vs. ugly situation makes for conflict or tension in a poem. Tension is what we've become accustomed to looking for.

It is the elusive nature of poetry, and the process by which it is written, that makes pinning it down to a statement of "my poetics" difficult. By the time I have decided on what that is (my poetic) it will have already moved on, and left me brushing off poetry-dust at the dead end of a one-way street. How do we know beauty when we see it? How do we feel a great poem when we read it? I've always subscribed to A.E. Housman's definition: poetry is words that affect us physically, that find their way to something deep inside that is obscure and latent, something older than the present organization of ourselves. When we connect with a poem, when the words resonate, reverberate, they connect us with the history of the human heart.

The Room Where They Found You

smelled of Madagascar vanilla.
After touching you for the last time
I scrubbed the scent from my skin - I would try
to remember later what the water felt like
on my hands but it was like trying to remember
thirst when you are drowning. They say love
doesn't take much, you just have to be there
when it comes around. I'd been there
from the beginning, I've been here all along.

I believed in everything: the hope
in you, your brokenness, the way
you arranged cut flowers on a tray
beside my blue and white teacup, the cracked
cup I'd told you brought me luck, the note
you wrote, "These flowers are a little ragged
- like your husband." The day you died

of an overdose in Vancouver
I found a moonshell in the forest, far
from the sea; when I picked it up
and pressed it to my ear I could hear you
taking the last breath you had the sad luck

to breathe. Our daughter cupped her hands
over her ears, as if she could stop death
from entering the life she had believed in
up until now. Childhood, as she had
known it, was over: the slap
of the breakers, the wind bruising the sea
tells her she is no longer safe in this world -
it's you she needs. I see you pulling away
while we stood crying on the rain-dark road,
begging you to come home. The vast sky
does not stop wild clouds
from flying. This boundless grieving,
for whom is it carried on?

BOBBIE **OGLETREE**

Bobbie Ogletree has had poems published in the following: the literary journal *Other Voices*; an anthology of emerging BC poets entitled *From this new world*; and a local magazine, *Sapiens*. One of her stories also appeared in the Federation of BC Writer's magazine, *Wordworks*. She has been a member of a women's writing group for almost six years. She and her partner live rurally in what was supposed to be an intentional community. That didn't work out, but she gets to look at a small forest from her writing room.

Breaking News tries to encapsulate the many voices I sift through in trying to make sense of the world's cycles of destruction and healing and our interconnectedness to all of it. This particular form, in which I have eliminated punctuation, allows the voices and events to overlap as they do in life. The mixture of the devastating, the mundane and attempts at spiritual sorting reflects what I consider part of the ongoing human dilemma. The form of the poem also gave it the rhythm I was looking for, a kind of breathlessness that requires coming up for air, much like the experience of the events and the news thereof.

Breaking News

krakow's museum of jewish culture and history used to be a synagogue
the kidneys and bladder are especially vulnerable in winter oh my god
my husband was on that plane osama bin laden rode out of afghanistan
on a white mare I don't know how she puts up with him a naturalist
gave a chicken some duck eggs the chicken sat on them and when
they hatched was not disturbed to find ducklings and later led them to
water fucking bastards will ruin the whole damn province abandon your
poverty mentality and visualize yourself wealthy from 1962 to 1972 the
us air force sprayed approximately 20 million gallons of defoliant over an
estimated 10 percent of south vietnam norton anti-virus is not enough
protection though sentient beings are numberless I vow to save them
all in my opinion with his kidneys osama bin laden is dead a few weeks
ago in minneapolis minnesota there was a lottery the winners got beds
in homeless shelters my religion is kindness at a factory farm a naturalist
found up to 5 hens squeezed into cages 12 inches by 12 inches I say
dispatch them to allah immediately george w bush really wanted to be a
baseball commissioner in arizona a woman died a few days after her 25
year old son was killed in iraq she couldn't stop weeping the newscaster
reported when a country is ruled with a light hand the people are simple
the price of crude oil exceeded 100 dollars a barrel today bring it on the
president said a saddhu in india kept one arm raised for 28 years for our
sins the bible predicted all this would happen this shall not abide we will
hunt them down and bring them in dead or alive they need potable water
food medicine immediately if a disaster of unequalled proportions is to be
averted we did not order this dessert

P.K. **PAGE**

P.K. Page writes poetry, essays, short stories and children's books. Porcupine's Quill has published her Collected Verse — *The Hidden Room* (Vols. I and II), *Planet Earth* (poetry), and two books of short fiction, *A Kind of Fiction* and *Up on the Roof*. U of T Press recently published *The Filled Pen* (essays). Forthcoming, *Jake the Baker Makes a Cake* (children), *The Old Woman and the Hen* (children), *The Essential P.K Page* and a book of glosas called *Coal and Roses*. She has received the Order of BC, the BC Lieutenant Governor's Award for Literary Excellence, The Banff Centre School of Fine Arts National Award. She is a Companion of the Order of Canada and a Fellow of the Royal Society of Canada.

A note about the *glosa*. It is a 14th, 15th Century Spanish court poem with strict rules. Its origin is a quatrain chosen from another poet's work. Each of its four lines launches a ten line stanza — backwards! That is, the tenth line is a line from the quatrain. That tenth line also sets the rhyme for lines six and nine. Do you really want to know this? Only a poet with a penchant for puzzles is likely to. For myself I have a love/hate relationship with form. A sculptor friend of mine used to work in stone or wood until she felt she was getting too tight. Then she switched to clay and worked until she felt she was getting too undisciplined. I think that is rather the course of my poetry.

How to Write a Poem

This poem is concerned with language on a very plain level.
Look at it talking to you. You look out a window
Or pretend to fidget. You have it but you don't have it.
You miss it, it misses you. You miss each other.
      John Ashbery — Paradoxes and Oxymorons

It is raining and you've decided you are going to write a poem.
What else is there to do besides phoning your mother?
And you don't feel like it not because you don't like your mother
in actual fact you love her and phone very often
but right now you have decided you are going to write a poem
and this poem will be a poem that you hope will be special.
Nothing symbolic or complicated, simple words, and language
a child could understand, but not a poem for children
with a moral and the struggle of good over evil.
This poem is concerned with language on a very plain level.

You are ready to begin. You have sharpened your pencil
the paper is lined in blue and is quite a bright yellow.
Listen to the poem talk, hear the words come together
and write them slowly and clearly so you can read them later.
This is the easy part, like taking dictation.
You must be deaf to long words like "crescendo", "diminuendo",
or cross them out if they surface, they are not for this poem,
and avoid scientific terms, botanical names or medical
and a musical vocabulary—"accelerando", "glissando".
Look at it talking to you. You look out a window

to avoid the poem's glance, turn away, embarrassed
by the poem and the fact that you're not fully attentive.
You are thinking of the rain that is beating with fury
against the dirty glass. You are thinking about everything
except the poem—about the gutters overflowing,
and is the cat in? But the poem begs you to give it
more than you are giving. The poem is expecting
your total attention. When it talks, you must listen.
Don't look abstracted—(o scribe, you must love it)--
or pretend to fidget. You have it but you don't have it.

It's not easy to focus.   Perhaps the plain language
is what makes it so difficult. This poem's elusive--
a flirt, comes and goes, takes back what was given.
(There are phrases that describe it but you don't want to use them.)
Now the wind has come up and the cedars are blowing,
the garbage lids flying like frisbees and either
the roof's sprung a leak, or you left the tap running.
The paper's still empty, the poem unwritten.
You would have done better to have talked to your mother.
You miss it, it misses you. You miss each other.

JOHN **PASS**

John Pass's poems have appeared in magazines and anthologies in Canada, the US, the UK and Ireland. Sixteen books and chapbooks of his work have been published, most significantly the four volumes comprising *AT LARGE: The Hour's Acropolis* (Harbour Publishing, 1991), *Radical Innocence* (Harbour Publishing, 1994), *Water Stair* (Oolichan Books, 2000) and *Stumbling In The Bloom* (Oolichan Books, 2005). *The Hour's Acropolis* and *Water Stair* were shortlisted for The Dorothy Livesay Poetry Prize (BC Book Prizes). *Water Stair* was also a finalist for the Governor General's Award. *Stumbling In The Bloom* won the Governor General's Award in 2006.

I know less and less of what I'm up to, or what use poetry might make of me.

Muse

Here it is then, the unmade poem, enormous block
of stone slung overhead, invisibly yoked to heaven,
or there behind me, somehow

winched in, elephant monolith in the room. To whom
might I appeal? Lord of the Doom Burden? Lord
of the Slick Surface nonchalance, of loose change
tossed on the side table, sliding, of the greased skids,
of the black ice lacquer that spins one

twice and makes a beginning of ending
up, facing elsewhere? Skittering thought. His terrible clichés.
No forward way. And that ice-cube brain, the brittle thinking.

I have months of notes, schemata, that belie a liquid center, a scrambled
yolk, the yellow lines on asphalt,

saltings. On this first beautiful morning in weeks. Winds
for weeks and the now stilled

trees, those sentinel, whole and broken, erect in frosted
eminence. All in a sunlight that's got me pleading no
depths please, no context, pleading no contest . . .

only what's worked up into seeing, verdant
edge of virgin forest, shimmer of sea, verbose and splashy
where everything's evident, nothing known, a bird, a flutter

of light at my shoulder. O Lady of the Lost Ways I knew
locus, nexus, your street address, the musk of your sheets.
Now stone chisel, ice-pick, lug-wrench, hammer
for the melting moment.

muse 2

read more says she in her white shift passing me

              leaf   leaf   leaf   leaf   leaf
a sprig, a broken branch branch branch branch branch branch leaf
              leaf   leaf   leaf   leaf   leaf

what can I do with this? plaintive, petulant, gruffly ahead I cast

it aside. it was

saskatoon maybe or ocean spray, smallish rough leaves serrated one
curled centrally reddish against its dark green edge

what can I do with this give me text

CHRISTOPHER **PATTON**

Christopher Patton's first book of poems, *Ox* (Véhicule), was a finalist for the 2008 Dorothy Livesay Poetry Prize. His poems have appeared in *The Fiddlehead, The Malahat Review, The Paris Review, FIELD, The Antioch Review,* and *The Western Humanities Review,* and have been anthologized in *The New Canon.* In 2000 he received *The Paris Review's* long poem prize. He has also published a story in verse for children titled *Jack Pine* (Groundwood). He divides his time between Salt Lake City, where he is a doctoral student in English, and Salt Spring Island, where he writes and tends to his apple trees.

I used to worry about the sentence and its elegance. How it might arrange, dispose, privilege, subordinate its elements with a sublime effortless grace. I say it but mean I. Someone, anyway, wanted to banish gravity, leave no trace of process, bring to a pleasing close what was rough and ongoing. My ethic assumed and created a gulf between the life and the work. One was inadequate and the other redress.

Those poems, or so I now feel, were loci of unreality, plates of lotus-meat, a Platonic republic where each thought sat cheerfully performing its assigned task. A will to order usurped the grains and textures of the given real. The ideal was a well wrought urn, shapely, self-contained, rich in pleasing ironies, irony being mystery, domesticated.

I dropped the urn on the floor. Made mosaics of the pieces, jagged, splintery, bloodied where they broke in or cut off. They framed a poetics of incompletion, of despair, which it would be the heroic work of the poet to overcome.

No one was interested in the breakage except me. And what on earth or under heaven could fit the description "incomplete thought" anyway? We call a sentence a complete thought, taking thought for propositional logic, even as our sentences, subject, verb, object, enforce divisions it would seem one work of poetry to undo.

No utterance, I now feel, no perception, no moment, is not entire. So no line is beholden to any other. A line is a being, not chattel, it lives in relation, not debt or service, to its neighbours.

A mind may be a fist or a loosening fist or an open palm. "The pine tree is perfect," writes Gary Snyder, and it's true. The word is, mind you, is redundant, the word perfect also.

Red Rock (1)

blue mug of wine of an evening
        perched on a burning stone
sagebrush & cedar, shed skirt of berries
heart impacted
            star in a stone cell

most of your work here idle, or ruinous
maybe you *should* go live with your father
end of the one life, end of the right world

Shih-pei, a fisherman, in his 30th year
left the river for the mountains and the Way
all the universe one bright pearl he said
        what's to understand?

        *

waterforms everywhere
                nowhere water
tremble   immobile
perched on a burning stone
      what have I given
      what have I not for

Red Rock (2)

heat a tin of red soup on butane
torn bread, cold butter, crumbs of chocolate
scent from the outhouse, wind swings about
    other people, they're ok

          *

Shih-pei set off down the mountain
struck his toe on a rock & drew blood
      this body is not so
      where's the pain from
jackrabbit, junco, scrub cedar
day & night negotiate the Way

shouts heard through a red wall
banging my head on the wall
      don't be afraid
      don't be angry with them

          *

drive home dark from a circus
mother draws us out of the car
Christopher, look up there
                our father looks too
more stars than we knew could be

Red Rock (3)

red & blonde sand
white stars at play

name of Kyushun, endless spring
plums astride the river blossom thinly
        I don't understand that about me

      *

gleam on cliff edge
            where just as before
Shih-pei drifts in a boat on the Nan-t'ai
not expecting a golden fish to strike

      *

you're forgiving
why not yourself

    wind and a square of mute
light where the shadows of willow branches
          all's unmasterable

SHAUNA **PAULL**

Shauna Paull is a poet, educator and community advocate. She completed an MFA in Creative Writing at the University of British Columbia in 1999. Since then, she has led creative writing workshops at the Shadbolt Centre for the Arts in Deer Lake Park, Burnaby, and at the Emily Carr Institute of Art and Design. In community, Shauna works together with migrating women for equality, mobility and labour rights. She recently led Poetry for the People workshops at the Rhizome Cafe. *roughened in undercurrent*, her new book of poems, was published in April 2008 by Leaf Press.

For me, poetry glimpses the common astonishments of lives lived at risk, the confinements of isolation, relational and state oppression and the persistent miracle of community. From its place at the juncture of witness and experience, poetry reaches toward where meaning may lie. Perhaps poetry also welcomes the sounds of the world into a body porous with listening and weaves our histories, ethnicities, visions, atrocities, resistances and hope, onto a page and beyond. Whatever wholeness we can make for each other in a world that is unnecessarily torn, there is poetry, listening through the din and the raucous talking heads of the present moment, working and working to re-ignite the sounds of justice and abundance. In my writing I am always indebted to the poetry of women gone before me, who have unearthed and sung the realities of our beautiful and complex lives, our diverse and too often individual struggles, our resiliences. I continue with them to work toward a world and a poetry that fuses political struggle with spiritual continuity and bridges us with our elders and our future.

curve of the world

now I give you to the morning
to the hushed almost blue space, tender
early leaves of the birch, the tiny sparrows.
even the breach of the power cables. I give you
our small-lit deck, tomatoes, verbena,
the desert daisies' open. closed.
open. even the newspapers' thudding,
hard noise and deceptions on doorsteps and the calm
ones who wake, shuffle to showers and toothbrushes,
oranges and coffee, jackets, backpacks,
the troubling curve of the world.
and the hidden ones –
underfuel for this city's arrogance, bent
at sinks in the back of restaurants, night-lit
offices, sewing machines, at berry canes
or missing, the ones gone missing –
if we could level a table round, enough.
until then,
I give you, my daughters, to each morning.
travel its muscular hope, its truculent damages
to the hot-heart quarry: pulse of a woman,
pulse of women. rest
and be gathered there.
and then go on.

GEORGE **PAYERLE**

Born in Vancouver of Hungarian parents, George Payerle escaped to the Sunshine Coast in 2001, having found the frenzied expansion of his home town no longer tolerable. Living in semi-rural Roberts Creek is already a lot more like living in postwar Vancouver than it is like the Roberts Creek of as little as forty years ago, but it's homey. Payerle is a novelist and poet. His books include *Unknown Soldier, The Last Trip to Oregon* and *Alterations*. His wife, Phyllis Surges, gardens, designs interiors, and teaches art. Their daughter, Bronwen, a visual artist and writer, lives in Vancouver.

Having been born an urban Coaster and now removed to life as a semi-rural Coaster, I view with dismay the depredations "civilization" is making everywhere. This is, like global warming, an inevitable result of human population growth and its unquenchable desire for the products of profit-driven manufacturing and real estate development. I still can't understand how Mother Teresa achieved sainthood in the public eye as well as in the eyes of Christians.

My dismay hasn't changed the focus of my interest in my work, but added a new note to the music of history I've always attempted to write. Being born twelve days after Nagasaki gives one a very particular take on the personal impact of world events and of the past. I grew up with veterans of the Second World War; hence my *Unknown Soldier* novel, a book which recreates the experience of an infantryman who survived, and returned to the civilian world he had, at least in his own mind, fought to save from dictatorship. He finds this world unwelcoming, difficult and in many ways repellant. But *Unknown Soldier* also bespeaks the ways in which many non-military people are veterans of unrecognized wars, domestic and foreign, in their daily lives. Most of my writing speaks of and for them.

Beatrix the Cat

killed by vehicle – a sorrow

Armload of catnip bloom
and petals of yellow iris
upon her smashed beauty
      curled like a blue furred chiton
we laid her under soil
and the blown poppies bend their broken heads
over her fresh grave.
Old Ludwig's Opus 131, written for
one instrument with four voices,
mourns
this little bright feline kindness
while the old boys,
arthritic gymnasts of the Oriental Shorthair school,
wonder at the smell of so young a death
laid down and freshened
for their more slowly dying nostrils.

Summer Solstice fragrance
amongst two violins, viola
and cello –
animals reminding us who we are,
youth and age with doors open wide
to the warm careless air of being.

SHEILA **PETERS**

Sheila Peters lives in Driftwood Canyon near Smithers in northwestern BC. Her poetry and fiction has been widely published in Canadian journals. *Tending the Remnant Damage* (Beach Holme, 2001) is a linked collection of short stories; *Canyon Creek: A Script* (Creekstone, 1998) tells the story of the eviction of a Wet'suwet'en family from its homesite near Smithers. Her most recent book, the *weather from the west,* is a collection of poetry and images published in collaboration with images by visual artist, Perry Rath.

Living here at the edge of the bush, I write poems to get up close to the old landscape, to search out the holy places that are all but invisible to us newcomers. By returning again and again to the same creeks and cottonwoods, by creating small paths with the pressure of my feet and my words, my poems bear intimate witness to the details of the land itself and the way it presses back upon us. At the same time, there are great forces being brought to bear upon these apparently insignificant corners of our planet and I make poems, as John Berger says, to place something substantial against the cruelty and indifference of the world.

Mung Beans
(for Bujji Govinda)

A widow, she hitched a ride home from the market.
A fruit seller.
Dalit.
Untouchable.
Two men in the cab of a truck. An old man on the bench in the back,
so she climbed in.

I would kill myself, she says, but what about my children?

The truck pulled over under a tree.
The driver and his companion told the other man to leave.
She knew then, she says, and she was afraid.
They spread her out on the hard bench
and did things to her for maybe an hour.

All rapes are the same, really, and each one is its own:
each man's whiskers a different shade of hard
each man's prick with its own insistent voice. One man's knees
got sore and so they took her outside to the soft ground under the tree.
When they ran out of things to do they looked for other utensils.
That's when she ran.

I pour mung beans into a jar and dust catches in the back of my throat.
I rinse the beans and pour the water down the drain
to find its way back outside into the ground.
The beans are not exactly round.
On one side there's an umbilical scar: the hilum.
Just below its white indentation,
the radicle. This is the nub of the first root.
Nosing its way toward moisture, it splits the dark skin.

Washed and washed and washed again,
the bean meat swells. We eat the sprouts: the pale root,
the first leaves' little flapping wings, and the dust from Bujji Govinda's feet
running through the tangled vines. Mung beans, she says.
They tripped her and she fell.

She is a loose woman, the policemen say, to be hitching a ride like that alone in the dark. What did she expect?

A Dalit.

Untouchable.

MEREDITH **QUARTERMAIN**

Meredith Quartermain's *Vancouver Walking* (NeWest, 2005) won the BC Book Award for Poetry. *Matter* is just out from Bookthug and *Nightmarker* is coming in fall 2008 from NeWest. She has given numerous public readings across Canada, in Toronto, Montreal, Ottawa, Windsor, Victoria, Edmonton, Calgary and Vancouver, and her work has appeared in many Canadian magazines, including *The Walrus, CV2, Literary Review of Canada, Prism International, The Capilano Review, West Coast Line, Windsor Review, Canadian Literature and Matrix.* She is co-founder of Nomados Literary Publishers.

Discovery has always been an important part of my work, writing into what I don't know, taking risks, giving up control. The workings of language, its possibilities and blind alleys, its illusions and dioramas, its other voicings from other times, the reverence or disgust we give to words – all these are my concern. I write to find out – to go to unanticipated places, unplanned vocalities. Humans live in words – these are our quintessential places. I'm constantly aware of the shifting geography of language, the contours, rifts, subductions, tectonic plates of the medium in which we exist. A sculpturing of our land-base has already occurred over the millennia of linguistic evolution and we too can erode it, or upheave it. We can also map it, write as cartographers.

A writer's work unfolds a life-time gestural impulse toward language, toward the imagined non-language world. A writer creates disturbances in the wind or the words, like the gestures of handwriting that carry our stamp unawares. I find it best not to try to control that too much, not to master it through rational thought, but rather tune in to the outside energy that's dictating through me, as Jack Spicer said, calling it Martians moving the mind's building blocks (i.e. its storehouse of language(s)).

Prose as a medium for poetry is particularly intriguing to me, as untrampled by literary convention. Poetic prose, as Charles Baudelaire noted, is not bound by the plot formulas of conventional fiction. It's an open territory which can include all the other genres. The poetic moves of rhythm, sound texture, image and juxtaposition can happen in prose along with dialogue and drama and narrative, and this makes for a rich, multilevel field of play.

Future Past

The past is coming. It's going to have arrived. The past will be a bed with no stead, its legs evaporous, its mattress imponderable. Perfect, imperfect, more than perfect, it will be tense. It will be going to have been tense. You'll sleep in this edgy. You'll make love in it. On its sheets, you'll find spots. You'll read books in it. Into it you'll be born and give birth. You'll make it and rumple it. You'll die in it.

The past is coming. It's going to have been eating and talking, talking and eating. It will be retroly progressical. Precooked, postcooked, and anticooked, the past will be your trophy. It will be succulently necessary. You'll waffle in it. You'll portion it out, even ration it. Milking its magpies, you'll soliloquize, and sandwich its muttering balbucinations in saucy falafels. It will butter you up; it will pickle you.

The past is on its way; it's going to have been coming. It will field, as in question. The past will crest and trough. Through its turbines, it will conduct inquiries and scoping zones. You'll rise and fall on its erections. In its sediments you'll corkscrew hither and thither. You'll dawdle, flit, halt, then dash, eke, linger, and saunter. The past will spread you out in thistles and clover, tides of neverness, everness, now a tussock, now a turf, now a clump, now a windrow, now a mouse, now a mole, now a snake, now a toad. Now the future is past.

HENRY **RAPPAPORT**

Henry Rappaport lives and writes in Vancouver where he co-founded Intermedia Press in 1968. He has four books of poems and an email list to which he sends new poems, henrap@shaw.ca.

I like most those poems that are deceptively simple and wonderfully moving. Poems of mine can surprise me with those qualities. And then I wonder where they came from and how they didn't get messed up. There is a danger of falling off the delicately beautiful tightrope I aspire to. If I fall to the sinister side, the poems can be too weirdly out there, and if to the right, too flat. And sometimes with good fortune, it just looks like falling, until you catch the tune.

There Ain't Nothin

for Karen Solie

Aretha sings there ain't nothin
like the real thing, and I agree.
A woman overhears,
wants to know what I'm singing.
I tell her and she says
nothing profound in that.
A picture on a wall
will not answer
when Aretha calls its name,
will not hold her
like his strong arms she sings to.
She is right about that too.

Then I wonder, her song in my ear,
if the real thing is her song,
that picture, the man or her longing.
I know they all are
but that's not what she sings.

When he was an infant
I held Benjamin in my arms
and we danced in the living room
of her song and as she sang
they all were: a man and a picture
of a man, a song and the singer
of that song, its writer, these
words and that infant in my arms.

KYEREN **REGEHR**

Kyeren Regehr (b. Sydney, Australia) spent many years in the world of theatre and dance, both performing and teaching. When she began her degree in Creative Writing at the University of Victoria she intended to study playwriting and fiction but was unexpectedly and completely seduced by poetry. Her home is in Victoria, BC with her husband and two daughters.

What happens when "there are no words" for something — what do we do with that emotion? When my mother developed cancer I started writing her a poem. I imagined that it would be inspirational, but instead "Preparing for Loss" poured out. It seems that a poem (or any art piece for that matter) finds a life of its own in the early stages of development. Many times I've begun a piece of choreography with a certain image or theme in mind only to have it transform into something entirely different. I've learnt to trust this, to let go of my ideas and allow the piece to go in its own direction; in theatre it's called "getting out of your own way." Interestingly, out of all the creative genres I've delved into, writing is the form in which I can most easily step aside. Sometimes it flows so smoothly that I feel like I'm cheating, that it can't be from me: I imagine a cache of writing that I'm somehow tapping into — but then it's time to edit.

At present I'm intrigued with how a poem finds its form, how it becomes a prose poem or a sonnet etc. and how that form encapsulates a particular energy or feeling that gives the poem its life. I want to discover more about line break — the weight or buoyancy, the tension or release it can generate. I'm obsessed with dropped lines and the way they create a doorway of afterthought. When we dance to music, it's as if the music opens up and allows us in — allows us to move through the "spaces" in the rhythm, in the notes: poetry can also be this immediate.

(The poem "Preparing for loss" is dedicated to my beautiful mother, Olga)

Preparing for loss

She can't help noticing the many things that come in pairs. She scrubs the faucets, slides her feet into work heels, rinses last night's wine glasses. Her menagerie of salt and pepper shakers line the window sill; a butterfly lands on the letterbox, folds its wings together. At work she makes jokes; *I'm actually having a boob job*. And in a sense it's true; they'll insert an inflatable bladder, stretch the skin slowly over several months.

Driving in the wet one evening she decides to take a detour through a strip of wilderness. The wipers squeak against the glass, turns begin to tangle in her mind. Two wild turkeys scuttle across the road and she slides to a stop at the edge of an intersection. The loose skin on their red necks jiggle; deflated balloons disappearing beneath the bushes. The headlights hold two spheres of rain— the left one flickers, then black. She turns the car around, drives back the way she came in the single beam of light.

D.C. **REID**

When he was three, D.C. Reid walked out onto the Alberta prairie and never came back. When he was five, he stuck his hand in a stream and pulled out a trout. Since that day his life has always been about water. Four books of poems have come his way, one novel and four books about fly fishing. His next two books of poems are: *You Shall Have No Other* and *Elegies*. His next non-fiction is *The Brains of Poets*, a book about the brain. When not at his computer, he is found most frequently in the wilderness of his Vancouver Island.

Years ago, I moved from the narrative lyric to the associative lyric, shepherded less and less toward meaning, even emphasizing the fragmentary. I set down what comes to me and ask what it wants to say. I am a raider of drafts and a grafter in the hopes the poems will grow as living tissue. I am a collector of quotes and do my best work when a little out of control, when my life is in chaos. Mentally, I use a page three feet wide because the conventional 6 by 9 is a tyranny of visual structure. My line is long, a completed thought. I write what intuition tells me, walking off the cliff with each new poem. For poems that crash I hope for a comfort for their brokenness. For the others, I am happy to have been granted the good fortune to have whatever gift there is for poetry. Once the poems are complete, I open my hands and they leave, to live their lives. They are not mine anymore, not mine to explain. Their meaning I leave to readers, I try to develop a new aesthetic with each new book. Poetry is a necessary love. Art is subversive, and you must be incredibly strong, and without ability to do any other thing than be an artist. It is scary, exhilarating, always falling forward — the act of falling and fear.

Where you are

You hear only the leaves when they turn away

The green backs of them disguising the threadbare distance

Disguising it with their thin green bodies that in their thinness
turn you to slumber

What you find there in the autumn is the silver of their leaving

They are the pigeons of the square in their washer-women clothes

The male in his circles the female of his attention

The silver is the lining of their green summer plumage

Then they are gone with the gold of your early eyes

Perhaps they are a market of fly-bitten dates

Perhaps the pigeons know that the green and their silver

Have always been the same but they do not hear

Your anguish that the sleight of hand of summer has you

On its wavelength between the flowers and the heaven

MURRAY **REISS**

Murray Reiss lives on Salt Spring Island with his wife Karen, a ceramic sculptor. He works as a freelance writer and editor and coordinator of the Salt Spring Island Water Council. His poetry and prose have been published in literary magazines and anthologies in Canada and the United States. His most recent publication is the chapbook *Distance From the Locus. He also performs as half of the folkenword/fusion duo Midnight Bridge with singer-songwriter Phil Vernon.*

Much of my misspent youth was misspent playing the pinball machines at the convenience store around the corner. For one nickel, if you were good enough, you could play all day, racking up one free game after another, the steel ball careening through the slots, bouncing off the bumpers, hitting the targets over and over, rolling down the flipper to that sweet spot where a flick of a finger sends it back to the top of the playing field to start all over again, while I throw in just enough body English to keep the ball in motion without making the machine tilt and thus shut down. This seems to have carried over into how I write a number of my poems — trying to keep that initial impulse moving as it tracks the careening motions of the mind bouncing off the people, plants, animals, events and news of my day, providing just enough guidance to keep the ball in play, without tilting the poem too far off its natural kilter.

The Last Day You Were A Child

If I gave you a mouse
on the last day of your childhood
and told you its whiskers
were my father's,
its eyes your mother's mother's,
and its fur the manes
of the horses that pulled
their wagons through Poland's swamps
would you press it to your heart
and stroke its fur?
Would you wish instead
I'd given you something shiny?

My father kept
his suicide a secret
until he guessed me
old enough and able
to guide his hopeless fingers
through the knots.
My mother
in her youth
tried to change the world.
Later, to make amends,
she embraced despair.

No one tells children the truth.
But you come from them,
these distant dead—you can't walk
around the block
without spilling their stories—
even though I never
properly introduced you.

Stroke its fur and
watch as its timid
whiskers
cease to quiver.

Hold it close
as you step out
into this world.

AL **REMPEL**

Al Rempel is currently an alternate teacher in Prince George. His poems have been published in *The Malahat Review, Grain, Reflections on Water* (on-line journal), in three anthologies: *Half in the Sun, The Forestry Diversity Project*, and *Down in the Valley* as well as in two chapbooks: *Sumas Flats and Black as Crow.*

Poetry is uniquely positioned to spend equal time in the visual and the aural; it's a place I like to be. My personal fable is that my pre-writing obsessions of photography and drumming inform both the optic and sonic qualities of my poetry. Look at them on the page. Read them aloud. There is this idea that form and content are intrinsic to each other, an idea that threads through Marshall McLuhan and goes at least as far back as William Blake. Most of my poems don't look like each other. I have to work hard to write a series. Place is important but how could it not be? It matters the most when you want to be here. What fascinates me is what's underneath. I don't just watch people, I watch people watch people. When a protestor and a politician are yelling on TV, I wonder if they were yelling before the cameras arrived. When people talk to me, I ask myself what they are saying. At times I see the thin edge of the universe waiting to be peeled back. Most times I refrain. The alleys reveal what the city is all about. Go ask the crows. If you live up north, ask the magpies what's going on. I recommend reading poetry if you enjoy looking. Attend poetry readings if you want to learn to listen. Start writing poetry only if you want to read well. Any talk of poetics makes me nervous. I learned from my fourth year in physics that the universe doesn't fit into formulas as neatly as we would like. Enter the bramble of life. Observe a thicket. Enjoy a poem.

Connective Tissue

I.

a stutter of Jake-brakes   a question of ridges   blue-eyed lakes
these narrow strands   railway, road, river   a single row of silvered cells
the roads feeding   an arena hides under tin   the sky cut clean
this two-arrowed town   foreign plates gone   due east or due west
a few fake blonds   there's a truck for everything   helpful intersections
an answer of back-roads   the first tinge of yellow   this soil packed with thought
freighting both ways   one restaurant no longer a statement   a chop-chop fall

if one could peer   the glacial push of till   land with little punctuation

II.

the frozen river   a narrow slit in the sky   boot-room door stuck open
the sound of knuckles cracking   a litter of 4x4's   the idle exhaust
orange garbage bags   a fuck-up of skidoo tracks   piles of thoughtless firewood
foot-prints pock-mark the yard   piss-yellow holes in snow   the shed out back
the sun makes a brief appearance   the train takes to counting   leaning flats
sickly-dark holes in the ice   the distant whine of a chainsaw   a reluctant spring

these ruts in the snow   moraine drifts underneath   always run in one direction

III.

a camper-trailer   faded orange stripe   clothesline running off
grown-over ruts   a smattering orchard   peaches, pears, apples
tufts of Kentucky Blue   a cherry that only blossoms   bees drone ancient code
falls out like a year of chemo   keeps guessing   as busy as RV's
a fruit-stand wears history thin   don't break or slow   a wet heartache
nosey tumbleweed at the fence   fresh fruit in new paint   slips of there
some-days the laundry's out   a bleach-boned roof   bras two sizes bigger
dresses that cast slimmer shadows   the colour of sage   slinks in at night

there's a constant hum   a noise bigger than   the air-conditioner falters

IV.

box-cars unmoved   shape-shifting clouds   trees taller than the town
the river slips under   the metal quietly ticking   store-awning, sidewall, asphalt
the great hulk of sky   a hard bright on the eyes   yawning mouth of a mine
creosote embedded in the air   a house with closed eyes   pounds on siding
slide from light to dark   squint of cumulus   shiver of curtains
horsetail scratches the underbelly   lazy circles   nodding tips of hemlock
a hawk drifts   tailings of the last gold rush   a thin layer of dust

the train clears its throat   theories of this or that   rails against the bedrock

V.

a house perches   shelter of cedar   the river churning up the darkness
uncomfortable against the tree   the sun on tip-toe   this drip-drip-drip
a lone crow with no comment   mist up the valley   distant hum of bridge-deck
a pick-up truck pregnant with boxes   white owl blinks   the resigned dog
spirits drift further back   the long exhale of a train-horn   settling dew on grass
echoes in the house   tall weeds around the edges   wafts of cigarette smoke

a wish of stars overhead   the river somehow quiet   an engine revs

VI.

plush carpet of grass   untidy hedge   the moss thick as banana slugs
fingers in gutters   a concrete sink on the lawn   seed-packets of flowers
the river throbs   sticky cottonwood buds   green streaks near the downspout
unflinching rush of traffic   a paisley couch on the porch   flush out the day
the mailbox knocked up under its chin   robins twitter   the sun reeks of green
the apple tree comes unhinged   curtains askew   scattered blossoms
a red truck owns the driveway   a stumble of stairs   this creaky old house
thick with windows   poplar moans behind the barn   too many rooms with beds

beyond the dike   raised above the lake-bottom   a train hitches and hitches

VII.

the river's tongue   open throat of a storm-drain   a snarl of blackberries
sea-salt on the tip   grass always green   overpasses caught in a shrug
nests of thrift-coats   crows scratch at the eaves   oil slicks under the dock
sun-glare   there's a sign for everyone   tracks lie down with the dandelions
a car on the shoulder steaming   seagull shit   the smog pierced through
strollers on the shore   neurotic waves   footprints hide behind logs

barely made out lines   a blue heron meditates   silt-plume, island, sky

HAROLD **RHENISCH**

Harold Rhenisch, co-editor of *Rocksalt,* is the author of twenty-one books, including *Living Will,* a translation of Shakespeare's sonnets into contemporary erotic English, the George Ryga Award-winning *The Wolves at Evelyn,* and Cross-Country Checkup Book of the Year, *Tom Thomson's Shack.* He is Robin Skelton's editor, the English translator of the postmodernist German playwright Stefan Schütz, a past winner of the ARC poem of the year prize, the winner of The Malahat Review Long Poem Prize for both 2005 and 2007, and 2nd Prize winner in the 2008 CBC Literary Prize for his long poem, "Catching a Snare Drum at the Fraser's Mouth." His latest book is *Return to Open Water: Selected and New Poems.* An active editor, reviewer and mentor, he lives in Campbell River, BC.

There is a poetry of British Columbia, distinct from a poetry of Canada or any other place. It rises from us, as we live within our history, on a land that is ours. For me, poetry has always been a spiritual path — at turns, material, practical, visionary, mythical, surreal, political and playful, but always animated by spirit. Music is increasingly a part of this path. I have found that music in various places: in the Sugarcane pow-wow, in the ragas on East Indian FM in Williams Lake (it has a range of about 3 kilometres), in small-town high school musicals, in Shakespeare, in the old gallows ballad tradition, and, most recently, in Bach's St. Nicholas Church in Leipzig, where Bach, and the church, played me. I am singing along.

Foetus on the Wawa Pedal

In those months I could make any face I wanted,
when I drank the moon's splishsplash 'til I turned blue,
my mother, my leaf-thin mama mia,
was a sweater over a pile of bones on a grassland hilltop,
dressed in her huffing breath. I tell you, that woman
was my iron lung. I said, *Mama, eat. We are too thin.*

Spring passed, with flowers, and summer
thundered my house. Mama's friends in the circus tents
of their dresses shelled peas, and weaver ants
climbed cherry limbs to the big top of the sky. I blew bubbles.
I made fish mouths, squealed squeaky kisses,
was seal and soda water. I was Elvis
hanging from a rearview mirror. I played Mom-to-be like a tabla.
I tied prayer flags to her spleen and her liver
and hiked down from the roof of the world.

I said, *Oh, Mama, I whale you. I breathe up a storm. I learned
what you had to teach me. I fall to the sea.* In those months,
I could pull back my lips in a tiger's snarl,
mouth words and word rivers of saffron and ashes.
Those months, Sailor Dad came into port again and again
with blue willow and trinkets; I traded cinnamon
and wild honey from the jungle for his clinker,
but there were no ragas, just elephants plodding in sawdust,
and the woman on the trapeze sitting up there shivering.

My lips sketched my face with a crayon in those days.
I drew my mother a cherry tree to climb down
to the iodine bunchgrass of the Columbia River.
I saw the ants take her in and make her their queen,
my beautiful mother with the black wings and the hourglass waist.
I saw the trout pour through my plutonium dreams.
I saw lips swim in my eyes like a thousand mouths,
each one swallowing a star; I saw the moon listening to ragas
on the radio while the wind blew through my mother's hair

like the sun through cottonwoods because this is her story,
not mine, and she forgot it in order that I could remember how to sing.

Oh, but now I have listened to ragas in the grasslands.
I have watched the snow fall on the earth
until the earth burned in a beaker. I have caught the smoke
in a retort and distilled it to a raindrop. I rained it
into the pool of my heart. The big trout in the dark
stirred under the old Green Mountain stage coach bridges.
What the trout said, I remembered. Oh, earth,
forget it to me now; forget it breathlessly:
all the pine trees are red in the Interior now,
and all the lakes between the Columbia and Srinagar
are drained of trout and this too is your story,
as surely as I die; we can speak that together at last.

Mother, with the same voice we can say, *As surely as I die,*
now I am the face I could not see. Now I am a fish.
I am listening to ragas of shine and smoke. I am dancing the chakras
of muscle and bone. I am climbing out of my own spine
one cell at a time. I am all backbone. Surely, you have seen
that the earth is only the raga of the mirror
broken across the heart's floor? Surely,
you are listening now as her rags weave you?
The singers are barefoot; they touch the earth's body,
and she touches the pedal, and waa waa waaa waa
goes the raga that is the earth's swollen cry.

AJMER **RODE**

Ajmer Rode has published books of poetry, drama and translation in English and Punjabi and his works are included in several English and Punjabi anthologies. His 1,000-page book *Leela* (co-authored with Bharati) is considered an outstanding work of twentieth century Punjabi poetry. *Rebirth of Gandhi,* his latest play, premiered at Surrey Arts Centre in 2004. He was on the National Council of The Writers Union of Canada in 1994/95 and is founding member of several Indo-Canadian performing arts organizations. The Punjab Government gave him a lifetime achievement award in 1994. He lives with his family in Vancouver, British Columbia.

When a sparrow chirps in glee or a dog howls in loneliness I hear poetry in its elemental form. I merely say it in words. Poetry is the core expression of life and of our lives. The words may assume familiar forms of verse or be embedded in poetic prose but without poetry the soul will curl itself into silence and rational mind will take over expression. Things will be useful or useless, good or bad, but no longer beautiful. With no experience of the beautiful, we would go insane. Poetry is as essential as love.

I grew up in village poverty in Punjab, lived next to city slums, and saw people fighting over half-eaten bananas. Even in North America where the scourge of poverty is lesser it is hard to escape the feeling of imprisonment by a system that breeds greed, encourages competition and exploits the environment ruthlessly. Poverty and exploitation have been etched deeply on my bones. Only poetry can bare the marks.

Blue Beaks

There was no temple around
and he didn't miss one
My father simply bowed
in the open and started working.

Every year he sowed wheat
in the dark brown soil
of Punjab

Before he buried the first seed
for his family
he took a fistful
scattered it and said
grow for the birds.

The second he scattered
for the wild animals, and the third
for the travelers who might
pass by and want to
nibble raw grains

Later when he
moved to the Fraser Valley farms
of British Columbia
Father picked blueberries

Sometimes
he paused took a fistful
of the fruit
hurled in the air and uttered,
this one for birds.

a whole bunch of song birds
ran riot in his head.
Beaks blue with half eaten berries

LINDA **ROGERS**

Linda Rogers is working on her bucket list. Every outrageous experience, whether it is jumping off a Turkish mountain or learning to tango way after her stale date ends up in a poem. She is married to mandolinist Rick van Krugel, who accompanies her lyrical adventures.

Don't ask me about prosody, because I am an anarchist in everything. My head is a big kitchen. I put my cooking pot under the part of the roof that leaks (the sky is falling), and wait for rain, maybe a star or two, possibly a crow. I have spices, lots of them, a pinch here a pinch there; I never measure. I add a song from the radio, a cup of sugar (everyone needs sugar), a squirt or two of milk, rose petals, honey, a headline from the morning paper, a naughty joke. Eggs. Lots of eggs. Eggs are the ultimate syntax. I worship the egg, kowtow to Brancusi. Always a footnote. I read while cooking, mix in the words. While I stir, I hum until I find the right key for the poem, a hook, a bridge. It's easy. Poems are gifts. The best ones are surprises; never to be repeated. Never use a recipe. Sonnet? Pissonit.

The Lilac Glove

You gave me the dead woman's
lilac glove; and the first thing I
thought about was the biology
teacher who told us how men and
women fit one another perfectly.
Like a hand in a glove, he said.
A month earlier you'd been sitting
on a Mexican beach, watching all
those beautiful men play in the surf,
both of you filled with a longing
for love in a warmer climate.

While the mariachi band rested
in the shade, you and the dead lady
may have heard snow falling on
the beach, the dead pianist traveling
south on a melting ice floe, playing
The Goldberg Variations on the
teeth of a nearly extinct species.

We all could see the dead lady was
enthralled with you. What is it with
people who chase impossible dreams
the way they also pursue summer
from one cold latitude to the next?

Our biology teacher said that desire
was a holy sacrament. The old lady
had a husband who made a child
with her the stormy night she'd filled
their room with lilacs as fragrant as
skirts worn by girls who dance in the
wind wearing nothing else. In China
they say the hand retains the scent of
a flower offered in love. This memento
does not belong to me. It belongs to
the daughter she gave away the year

she went crazy for sunlight. I will put
this poem inside the glove and send
it to her so that she might smell the
lilacs her mother picked in the rain
the night the wind blew her down.

RACHEL **ROSE**

Rachel Rose's first book, *Giving My Body to Science*, (McGill/Queen's University Press) was a finalist for the Gerald Lampert Award, the Pat Lowther Award, and the Grand Prix du Livre de Montreal, and won the Quebec Writers' Federation A.M. Klein Award. Her second book, *Notes on Arrival and Departure*, was published by McClelland & Stewart in 2005. Her short story, *Want*, won the Bronwen Wallace award. Her poems and essays have appeared this year in three anthologies: *White Ink, Double Lives,* and *Between Interruptions*. Rachel was born in Vancouver, where she now lives with her family, after living on Hornby Island, BC and in Anacortes, WA, Seattle, Montreal and Japan.

I write out of hope and sorrow and curiosity. I write because the world is hard to bear when we open our eyes. I write because we are all connected. We are all connected: my truest identity is as a writer, a poet, because I am able to forge links with people all over the world who live utterly different lives than the one I have chosen, and who also value creating, witnessing, praising and observing the world and our place in it with care, as a mother does, as a lover does.

What the Sea Perhaps Heard

Killer whales hunt a blue whale calf
and eat his tongue. As he bleeds to death,

blood seeps without a sound into my body.
The gulls come, screaming their belly-greed,

the small fish come with their needle teeth.
The mother blue has more grief

In her massive body
than anything else I have held.

No one has seen what I see: how the great white sharks
copulate, fitting together in secret method.

 And when the octopus siphons me inside her,
and I unfurl her delicate legs with warm currents,

she blushes for me alone. I hold the tight curl
of the seahorse's tail as he pivots,

protecting his basketful of life.
Observe the spaghettini arms of starfish

reaching for drifting food. Hear their little song:
the stomach, the stomach! Dear urchins, sweet limpets.

All feast in me. In the heat of my armpit
waves curl their black seaweed, stones groan

as they are ground to sand. I rock them.
In my cold brain I am rational,

I do not weep to feel the polar bears
scrape my frozen cheeks.

I do not weep when the belugas
sing or narwhales leap like unicorns

and when icebergs collapse I am
scraping dead skin from my forehead

so I can think better, that thunderous, cleansing
crash. Sometimes I catch your broken boats

and your broken bodies, your diamond necklaces,
your New World apple trees, I accept everything,

I turn no one away. That's me gripping your line, your net,
your boots in invitation, dragging your thighs as you run.

At dawn the grey whale fills his baleen
with a noise like water falling through feathers

and at dusk you sail your boats
across my belly, dragging your hands

as you stare into the wet green silk, like a child looks
under his mother's dress again and again,

thinking she won't notice, to see
where he came from.

JOE **ROSENBLATT**

Joe Rosenblatt was born in Toronto in 1933. He became interested in writing through his association with the worker poet Milton Acorn in the early sixties and the metaphysical poetry of Gwendolyn MacEwen. His first book of poetry was published in 1966. He has written more than 20 books of poetry, several autobiographical works and his poems have appeared in over 30 anthologies of Canadian poetry. He received the Governor General's Award for poetry in 1976 and the BC Book Prize in 1986. Several bilingual volumes of his poetry has been published in Italian and translated into French, Dutch, Swedish and Spanish. His most recent poetry volume is *Parrot Fever* (Exile Editions, 2002). He lives at Qualicum Beach on Vancouver Island with his wife Faye and their three cats.

Poetry is going out on a blind date to meet your soul at some trendy café on Commercial Drive in Vancouver's East End. You end up sitting at an empty table waiting for your true essence. You don't realize that your date is sitting at the next table drinking some bubbly white Okanagan wine. The waiter gives you a menu. He is a cadaverously lean vegan type. "What's on tap," you ask the poker-face waiter. He reads out the brand names of some brews made at a micro brewery on Salt Spring Island. You note a snootish tone in his voice as he lists the two available brews on tap. " We have," he says, "Eternal Life, a fuzzy dark ale, and Deep Space, a sparkly bitter stout." Suddenly, just as you are about to try Eternal Life, your waiter fades away. Not only do you have an unbelievable thirst, you're still alone. You stare down at your navel still wondering if your date will turn up. That's poetry!

Water

I am a meandering body of a spirited lake
Carrying minnows of fleeting thought
Stranger, your artificial flies have no sex appeal.

For what I perceive are emaciated wings
and laughable torsos shamelessly floating;
Select a few meaty voluptuaries dressed in gold
From your wicker basket, cast them out to me!

Starved for iridescence seasoned by a piquant musk
A larvae- fed soul cries: 'See, there's my hunger caught on a riffle;
Fetch it quickly lest it be mistaken for a waltzing stonefly
and vaporized by some mottled nibbling phantom.'

Striding in leaden hip waders, evening fast approaches
Wearing the sky for a hat bedazzled with baubles.
He's there to encircle us all in a wide invisible net
We're not his guests, but his meal served on a misty table.

RHODA **ROSENFELD**

Rhoda Rosenfeld was born in Montréal in 1942. She grew up during "La Noirceur" and came of age with the Quiet Revolution. Formed in Montréal, she was transformed by meeting artists and poets who came from the west in the mid '60s. She arrived in Vancouver in 1968. Since that time, she's been a participant in the visual arts and literary communities there. Among the venues at which she's exhibited are the Contemporary Art Gallery, Artspeak and the UBC Fine Arts Gallery. Her work (both visual and literary) has been published in *West Coast Line, Raddle Moon, Front Magazine* and *W*.

Poetry is when words don't fail me or maybe it's more accurate to say, it's the passionate utterances that emerge out of deep silence when they do.

a short intervention into the long poem (fr. EFfari)

Clip 16

(and again at the table)

Wince: Forced into language, I had to transgress its spreading neuronal rush
in search of the new borderline.
By then, I'd seen his brother sleeping. But I also knew by then that Canada

      is

        Close with no cigar.

Evince: And that Psychology is a combustion of emotions and language,
Even if you didn't have any.

Invincible: I'm nourished by having to eat my words.

Incipient: Try mincing the word trestle.

Wince: I regret being too dumb for rebarb.

Evince: Poetry is when words fail me.

Convince: Of the wolf clan, maybe coyote.
Naw, wolf.

Evince: Ciliated epithelia.

LAISHA **ROSNAU**

Laisha Rosnau grew up in Vernon and has since lived in Tofino, Kelowna, Victoria, Vancouver and Prince George. Her work has been published in magazines and anthologies in Canada, the US, Australia and the UK. A chapbook of her poems, *getaway girl*, was published by Greenboathouse Books in 2002. The same year, her first novel, *The Sudden Weight of Snow*, was published by McClelland and Stewart. A full-length collection of her poetry, *Notes on Leaving*, was published by Nightwood Editions in 2004 and won the Acorn-Plantos People's Poetry Award. She lives in Prince George with her husband and their son.

I like reading and writing poems because they are not statements. Poems are words on a page, arranged in a way they have never been before. How we experience them is up to us and changes with every reading. For me, both the poems I write and those I read are a living archive, a leap of faith, and a reason to pause and pay attention to that page, those words and the space around them.

I've Got You: August 1981

1.

Temperature mounted until it became a body
of heat, crush of weight holding us down.
Weather reports looped – *it is getting hotter
and hotter* – and news became a tally
of missing children, ten in less than a year.
They would be found hoarding the cold,
clutching it in ditches, ravines, groves of trees
so thick they held perpetual dusk by day,
wholescale darkness by night.

2.

We were not allowed outside alone, discovered
it was finesse, not force, that was needed
to play ping-pong properly, squeezed
the plastic balls instead, their *pop*! so satisfying.
Wanting something cooler on our palms,
we helped each other reach the exposed
pipes, underbelly of the hotel, and swung
until we were swatted off by staff,
ordered back to our room.

3.

Our mother on the bed, face shrouded
with a wet cloth folded up
off her mouth. Our father stood,
Scotch in hand, staring down
the television. *Sick bastard*, he said.
When our mother got up and passed by
the screen flickered, smeared the fabric
of her slip. *They caught him,*
she told us, *we'll all feel better now.*

4.

Yorkshire pudding steamed when opened
so easily, the roast beef caught in the teeth
of our knives, not as rare as we wanted.
Indulged, we were allowed any kind of drink,
ordered Shirley Temple and Roy Rogers
to the table in frosted glasses, submerged
maraschinos bleeding bright. The Big Band
played Sinatra covers, doors open,
sounds tossed across the pool, back again:

I've got you under my skin, laughter, splintering
glass when the drink slipped from my hand,
calves cool before the liquid dried
to the kind of sticky that comes with sweetness.

GREG **SIMISON**

Greg Simison is a poet and playwright living in Vernon, BC. He has published three volumes of poetry: *Disturbances* (Thistledown Press, 1982); *The Possibilities of Chinese Trout* (Okanagan College Press, 1986); and *What The Wound Remembers* (Borealis Press, 1993). In 1999, Really Small Vernon Press released *The Moon Road,* a chapbook version of a story commissioned for stage presentation. For the past fifteen years, besides composing plays, Simison has been writing the great Canadian novel. He is currently still attempting to complete page three of that magnum opus.

I spend little time analyzing the intellectual process of writing poetry. This comes from a fear of hexing myself — look too closely at something and you can lose your focus. Write with gut/revise with the brain is the only rule I acknowledge. The "gut" part of that rule is the most dominant, and, as a result, after writing ten drafts of a poem I frequently find myself ending up with a final version that most closely resembles the second draft.

As a Canadian writer I'm somewhat uncomfortable confessing that the two contemporary poets I admire currently are both American: Billy Collins and Ted Kooser. I respect their successful attempts to write a kind of poetry of place and how they interact with the natural environment of that place. It's a pattern often followed by BC poets, and impossible for most of us to ignore when we live where the geography is so dominant.

Kootenay Lake

This lake seldom surrenders its dead—
glacier fed, as cold in pockets as the North Atlantic,
only mild surprise would greet the arrival of an iceberg
in the bay at Kaslo one morning.

Clumsy fishermen, broken prospectors,
deck hands blown from sternwheelers, drift
perfectly preserved between thousand-year old trees,
slowly sinking as they turn to stone,

eventually joining other legends—
trout, as long as a liar can spread his arms,
sturgeon that swam with dinosaurs, and drowned mammoths:
prehistoric deadheads as fresh

as any lifted from permafrost.
Accept these as possible, then anything is possible—
living dragons, sasquatch roaming the steep shoreline,
ghost ships plying night waters.

'The stuff of poets and barflies,'
some scoff, insisting a sudden glimmer in the depths
is simply a lost fishing lure, or play of light on broken glass,
anything but a watch chain dangling

from an old-fashioned vest,
or the glint in a frozen eye. But no matter on which side
of the argument they fall, cold or superstition restrict swimmers
to the warmer shallows,

keep older, wiser fishermen
trolling only the lake's thin skin— the deeps the preserve
of foolhardy night-lampers, unaware of what grim catches rise
to their small, bobbing moons.

PETE **SMITH**

Out of Coventry, England (1947), exilic (1974) & idyllic enough among pines, aspens, ospreys, kestrels, red-necks & bikers at 3000' at Pinantan Lake, BC. Tiny dot on the word map courtesy of Wild Honey Press, *Poetical Histories, Tinfish*, above/ground press, *The Gig, Agenda, jacket #9, Crayon #5, The Capilano Review, The Paper.* A chapter forthcoming in The Salt Companion to John James (Cambridge, UK). Other stuff elsewhere. Has a weekly poetry radio show, Viva-Voce, on CFBX 92.5 at TRU, Kamloops, Wednesdays 1-2 pm.

I write poetry to find out where the boundaries were. If self is the bone & connective tissue, and poetry is the blood-flow, then self-expression is a mere reading of the pulse. Occasionally it's important to know your pulse rate, but there's so much more to life/poetry than that. Perspective fails often: in the beginning was the number, followed by aeons of inconceivable energy & stuff, late in the day word strutted onto the scene, attempted to clean up & hijack the glory. Still, word is the best way to you from me & vice-versa. Language at a certain pitch will obliterate self, but if then trusted well enough can conjoin self's warring clans, self & other (person, place, creature, idea etc.) at astonishing levels. I don't know if I'm shaping the poem or it me, but I want to be open to the richness of outside, the beyond-us: the riches of the worlds of the human, other creatures, tame or wild, those slow cousins, trees, rocks, sand. Word came late in the day & owns nothing. But finally I can disown through word (all excess ambition) & get on with my tasks: to listen to the listening world; to voice all the cries the human is capable of, utterly.

Prerogative

We gather under the banner of plurality & wait for
trickle down – as if we was a pyramid, I a dividend

As residual tickles pleasure down our collective
past is, we declare, an open & shut mummy

If it's all the same to you, with your penchant
for song, we'll take the descant & run

Kingdom came reigning down on Boswell Field –
one end of the panto horse unzipped a wicked grin

A ghazal does not give room for us to stamp
our authority, lick our prerogative, frank our maleness

We lack luster but make up for it with
shine – always the reflection never the source

Vertigo, he said, is the only way to go. Vortex,
she said, we have the horizontal & we're holding

One gender, solo, created an onanian agenda
kept the minutes for years but slid into as usual

We lather under the banality of plura – there's
safety in numbers, but First Kings is a torture

As one who has sired but never harboured, seeded
but not enfleshed, I'll assume the position. Outside

At the tap-tree of osmosis we hold our breath
to be self-evident, enough for one constitution

A host of feathers in a down of Pentecost
flaming imposters burn us at every turn

RON **SMITH**

Born in Vancouver, Ron Smith is the author of four books of poetry, two works of fiction, a play and a children's book. In 2002, a selection of his poetry was translated by Ada Donati and published in a bilingual edition in Italy. He lives with his wife, Patricia, also a writer, on Vancouver Island. He received an honorary doctorate, D. Litt., from UBC and was the inauguaral Fulbright Chair in Creative Writing at Arizona State University. His children's book was a finalist in the 2008 Illustrated Children's Book category of the BC Book Prizes.

How to speak of poetry, of ethereal, imaginative leaps? For me, poetry is a way of seeing and hearing the abundance of the world we live in. On occasion this may be a political act; invariably it is a process, ideally never merely reactive or referential. When a poem is working, a rare occurrence, it has the feeling of revelation and awe, as if something hitherto unknown has been exposed or unearthed. Breathed in. While this explanation may sound precious, if the language, whether reasoned, raving mad or lyrical, has led you to a fresh place, to the heart, where dance and music surprise, then you hope you have touched not only your own life but the lives of others. All of this shifting and digging within the language, attempting to find the right register, is a matter of discovery, love and bliss. It is also a part of our history, our archaeology. But mostly it is rooted in the moment in which the poem illuminates lives lived and felt in what Auden calls the "fallen world."

In Time

Beyond the kitchen window, in the meagre light
Of a winter's day, earth and bud begin to swell.
Inside, things left unsaid
Intrude. Once again we are burdened by
This fickle silence, the distractions of percolating
Coffee, the day's chores, split wood.
So easy to be misunderstood, to hold
Longing in mind, to feel unattended,
Frozen, against this emptiness. And so easy
To lose yourself in another's expectations—
Or in the weather. How different
Our moods are, she says,
When the rains come—and I'm caught
By the way stillness curves
Through the glistening garden
Cutting light into shadow
Like a crow's wing.

In time, perhaps, we learn to trust
In love, the inevitable seasons, trilliums,
The pungent smell of a morning fire.
In time, we surrender promises
To the moment; breathing the fallow earth,
We remember how we were
Before these words, these quickening days.

DAVID **SWANSON**

David Swanson has had poetry, fiction and non-fiction published in Canadian magazines. He is a student in the Optional Residency MFA at UBC and was the co-winner of *Event* magazine's creative non-fiction contest for 2007. He lives on Gabriola Island.

Dennis Lee said it all: poetry occurs when the "thrumming" happens. That's what poetry gives me — an out-of-body, out-of-mind moment in my life when boundaries soften, and dark things slip into the light, and white roots pull out of the soil. As far as form goes, Brian Brett (with help from Hass and Gluck) helped me begin to understand form in a larger way than issues of meter or rhyme: I have started to search for what lurks behind the words, the defining shape of the music against which local departures occur. I am also playing with open-field poetry, which I have written before, but which I think I'm now writing with better understanding of the choreography that the page offers.

March Morning

This morning the sun sliced through the dew
that washed the greenhouse windows. This morning
the grass was wet, like an ocean, like a beach,
like a dream fresh from the white roots, the black earth.

This morning my coffee was cold and bitter dark.
I counted my losses on fingers, on toes;
yet the numbers were more than this,
the dead friends who dance in the darkest shadows,

who sift like the fog that slipped over today's first sun.
This morning I traveled the tide pools of August,
where memories scuttled like crabs under eel grass in the bay.
Here, I said, and here, the secrets of anemone, of stone.

I heard a door close in the middle of a forest, an earlier time.
I heard a young girl singing. Her voice in the fog scattered,
became quiet, became unconcerned about anything
beyond itself—working like thread to its edges, to its seam.

The alpacas brayed in their paddock next door,
consumed by their coupling, their diet of rotted apples, while
outside my window one jay pecked another; two pairs of claws
rose into the air, each bird screaming it is me, me, me.

Later, the sun skinned the morning's wet filament,
one layer at a time, while it tip-toed back inside my garden,
all wide and golden, filling each window, each room,
with light, touching my arm like a child's shy hand.

ROB **TAYLOR**

Rob Taylor was born in Vancouver, raised in Port Moody, and now, after a number of travels, again lives in Vancouver. He is the co-founder and editor of *One Ghana, One Voice*, Ghana's only poetry magazine. His poems have appeared recently in *Antigonish Review*, *Dalhousie Review and Vancouver Review*.

I am interested primarily in the intersection of poetry, history and place. Still a young poet, I have spent much of my time writing on distant places, and have produced two chapbooks inspired by the histories and peoples of other parts of the world (China and Ghana, specifically). Having recently returned home, my writing is now focused on Vancouver, its people and its stories.

Grey Diamond Wallpaper

Just before the anesthetic set in, she whispered *wait*,
so he did.

His neighbours brought him fresh clothes and blankets.

Whenever one of the ward's patients was removed
the nurses offered him the leftover dinner tray.

On the third day they let him bring a couch in from the waiting room,
though this changed little.

To pass the time he spoke to her, softly describing
the comings and goings of the nurses,
the facets of the room
(the grey diamond wallpaper,
the clock with the jammed second hand,
the flattened bottle cap he'd attempted to repair it with).

He tried once to finish a crossword puzzle, but gave up in frustration.

He came to the conclusion that he hated the English language
for all its ambiguous words.

He asked for a language of clarity, where *still* referred only
to the continuation of things and *wait*
meant she'd be coming back soon.

RUSSELL **THORNTON**

RussellThornton has published four books of poetry, *The Fifth Window* (Thistledown, 2000), *A Tunisian Notebook* (Seraphim, 2002), *House Built of Rain* (Harbour, 2003), which was a BC Book Prize finalist and ReLit Award finalist, and *The Human Shore* (Harbour, 2006). He won first prize in the League of Canadian Poets National Contest in 2000. For a number of years he divided his life between Vancouver and Aberystwyth, Wales, and then Salonica, Greece. He now lives where he was born and grew up, in North Vancouver, at the foot of the mountains on the north shore of Vancouver's Burrard Inlet.

My whole life, I've had in my ears the local rain sounds, the creek and river sounds and, of course, the seagull cries. I've imagined I could hear the tree presences, not only as wind moved through them, but as they drew water up through their trunks. I've watched the rainclouds glide across the rooftops, the river-mist pour down the river canyons. I've watched the air light up as if for the first time after rain. I find I write about a number of subjects, but I can't help but feel that it's the setting of the North Vancouver area that inhabits and informs most significantly whatever imagination I possess. It seems inevitable that in writing a poem, I'll use details that originate in the local non-human environment. It's an environment full of movement, quick change and pure vitality, and it incites transformative inner experience. For me, an authentic poem is a kind of stored vitality and, to paraphrase Robert Graves, a poem is stored magic. When I read illustrious poems I feel that they work inexhaustible magical effects. They deliver a controlled shock of pleasure and delight, summon up an alertness and, like the mountain, forest, mist, cloud, creek, river and rain energies of my locale, prompt transformation, over and over. The poetic high points of the language — those acts of supreme verbal music, thought and feeling — seem to me to be miraculous everlasting imaginative events. They call forth as in the instance of the psalmist writing, "Deep calleth unto deep..." They rouse us to attentiveness as when William Blake cries out to the "sleeper" to "awake! expand!" I think a true poem also allows human consciousness to join, at least fleetingly, in the natural world's wider, multifarious, ongoing poem of the unfathomable.

Nest of The Swan's Bones

She will build a nest of the swan's bones...
— Robinson Jeffers, *Shiva*

for Tim Bowling

High in the blue air above the dumpster in the back lane,
between the mountains and the tidal flats,
on the thermals and updrafts a summer hawk does slow turns.

The crows pick at the waste on the asphalt.
The men push jingling shopping carts. They mimic life
in a prison yard. The wild white swan is dead. Where I caught

trout as a child, no trout swim now. The drives
and crescents gouge ravines, make creeks disappear. Where wild
baby fish run, they run gauntlets of penned fish. Are eaten alive,

eyes popping out as sea lice eat right through their heads.
The hawk dances. Circles, dances. Its shadow flits
unnoticed across men, spreads over a rodent or bird

it dives to, inserts claws into, and clamps large feet on, stomping it
as if beating time. It splays flesh and flies
away with it into the sunlight. The hawk takes up an owl's hoot

and a sparrow's last chirp, a heron's bill-snap and a smelt's silence,
into its disinterested scream. The swan
glides in beauty in the hawk's sight, and fills all the hawk sees

with brilliant, blinding whiteness. Moment by moment,
the men go back and forth. They search out what they trade
for a full bottle or syringe or pipe. In my room with the lit up screen,

I lie and dream my dream. I feel it must also be God's,
this dream of the person of persons. Where the dream comes through,
it punctures me, and I breathe dark air. The air thuds

into pockets like a plummeted elevator. Oh monster home. Oh
specialty wine outlet. Oh auto mall. The wild white swan
is dead. The hawk hunts and kills the swan for love. It will build a new

nest of the swan's bones. It will keep this nest unseen.
I am a person, I soil the cage in which my heart flings
and flings itself against the bars, I try to own

the view of every murderer, and yet I try to sing
the way out through the hawk's claw holes to the repose
in the nest of fire at the tip of the hawk's wing.

PETER **TROWER**

Born, England, Aug 25, 1930. Emigrated to Canada 1940. Worked at many trades, mostly logging. Published books: *Moving Through Mystery* (1969); *Between Sky and Splinters* (1974); *Alders and Others* (1976); *Ragged Horizons* (1978); *Bush Poems* (1978); *Goosequill Snags* (1982); *Slidingback Hills* (1986); *Unmarked Doorways* (1989); *Hitting the Bricks* (1997); *Chainsaws in Cathedral* (1999); *Ship Called Destiny* (2000); *There Are Many Ways* (2002); *Haunted Hills* (2004). *Prose: Rough and Ready Times* (1993); *Grogan's Cafe* (1993); *Dead Man's Ticket* (1996); *Judas Hills* (2000). Awards: BC Book Award, 2000; Terasen Lifetime Achievement Award, 2002; CAA Award, 2004. CD's: Sidewalks and Sidehills, 2003; Kisses in the Whiskey, 2004 Upcoming: *Smeltertown* (poetry); *Pages From Life-Log* (short stories).

I think of myself as a storyteller just as much as a poet and almost all my work is drawn from real life experience. I started out as a rhyming poet in the mode of Robert Service but soon graduated to free verse and other modern forms. I first gained critical attention for my logging poetry and have published several collections on this subject. My three novels also draw from these woods experiences. Lately I have been branching out into other subject matter. My late partner, Yvonne Klan, introduced me to the legends and lore of the early fur trade and I am presently working on a series of poems inspired by this fascinating material. I have not entirely given up rhyming verse but now apply it to song lyrics only.

Ghosts of The Baseball Days

for Yvonne

Woebegone enclaves of yesterday
they straggle wearily out along the CNR's East Line
following the Fraser River:
from Prince George to Tete Jaune Cache
a wounded battalion of faded names -
Giscome Hansard Penny Dome Creek
Snowdhoe Goat River McBride Dunster -
dwindling echoes of palmier boom times -
busy halcyon days when thirty active sawmills
whined and clattered beside the railroad tracks
cranking out lumber and prosperity

Broken ruin of a powerless power house
rears raggedly up from a stranglehold of bushes -
vacant patch of grass mopes beside the highway
where, years back, a railway station stood -
a thriving community flourished -
huge half-collapsed building looms across an unmowed field
once the company manager's house
later a dairy farm for the townsfolk and mill workers
finally just just another crumbling relic -
abandoned ball park offers only weeds and memories
to the phantom crowds in the sagging bleachers

Ghost towns soon-to-be ghost towns totally-vanished towns -
the mill still clanks away at Upper Fraser
but it too is doomed to close forever in a month -
the townsite was bulldozed and burned two years back -
a solitary cafe, ironically named Paradise, still remains -
soon it will stand alone when the sawmill is dismantled -
"Guess we'll try to keep going somehow," the lady owner says bravely

Depression recession repossession
have plagued and pillaged the forlorn East Line -
somehow, most poignant of all are the abandoned ball parks -
once almost every town had its own team -
companies often hired men for their playing skills alone -
but those lost communities contest on the diamonds no longer -
gone like the sawmills that sponsored them are the carefree baseball days.

ED **VARNEY**

Ed Varney earned his MA in English Literature at Syracuse University where he studied with American poets Delmore Schwartz and Donald Justice. He came to Canada in 1968 as a draft dodger and lived in Vancouver for 36 years. He founded Intermedia Press in 1969, The Poem Company (with Henry Rappaport) in 1971, and The Poem Factory (with Carolyn Zonailo) in 1991. He was a founding member of Artropolis in 1987 and served on the board of numerous arts organizations. He has edited several poetry magazines and has published three books of poetry and a dozen chapbooks as well as appearing in many literary mags and zines. In 2004 he moved to Courtenay on Vancouver Island where he intends to spend the rest of his life in relative obscurity.

Poetry is not song, not rhymes, not versification, not poesy, not linguistic gymnastics, not language cleansed and purified, not a lyrical expression of what's bothering you, not a hodgepodge of trite truisms and trivialities, not a clever play on or with words, not correct or proper grammer, syntax or spelling, not iambic, dactylic, spondaic, trochaic or anapestic, not prosody, not doggerel, not the sublime longings of the imagination, not a heartfelt plea for understanding or sympathy in a world where no one cares, not a panacea for the emotionally distressed, not off the top of your head, not verbal diarrhea, not a method or a discipline, not work, not the prophetic ramblings of a madman, not the product of a personal connection with a fickle muse, not a narrative, not the fire of genius, not a situational linguistic event, not a compendium of what everyone and his dog have felt or feel, not fast, smooth, pleasant, friendly, pretty or sweet, not a spontaneous utterance of whatever is on your mind, not easy reading, not a good career choice, and not very interesting to most people who are not poets.

Things I've Said

Inside our skull,
each of us speaks
our own language.

The distance between us
is an illusion, an illusion
validated by experience.

Thinking is burning holes
in my mind - too painful to continue,
too awful to stop.

Inside my skin I'm a young man
who doesn't believe he's getting old.

Climbing a ladder to see the stars
doesn't get you any closer.

Everywhere on the earth
it's the same sun, same moon.

The beginning of time was not long ago.
Before then everything just was
but it had no name.

You can't move fast enough
to outrun your past.

Money is just arithmetic.

Opposition keeps the edge
of the blade sharp.

The present is the only place
you ever feel anything.

Tomorrow never comes.

ANN GRAHAM **WALKER**

Ann Graham Walker is a journalist, a former CBC current affairs radio producer, and a former speechwriter to NS premier and humanitarian, Dr. John Savage. She's had poetry published in *PRISM International*, the *Gaspereau Review, Pitkin Review*, the *Windfire Anthology*, Leaf Press's Monday's Poem series, and two chapbooks edited by Patrick Lane: *All that Uneasy Spring* (2007) and *A Small Grace* (Fall, 2008). She is a graduate of Goddard College's MFA/Creative Writing program, and is currently working on her novel about growing up in 1950s Argentina, *The Girl in the Garden*.

I have spent my writing life as a print journalist and CBC radio producer; my poetry lived in dresser drawers and old notebooks. That's probably the safest place for it – but when I moved to BC in 2002 I decided to step right into the danger zone. The crafting of a poem is an all-important midwifery of cadence and sound. The poem itself is a powerful, ancient impulse to name what is here. I am very reticent to analyze how it happens. Poets' words have become critically important in these disturbing and rapidly changing times. I think the next danger zone that I will explore is a deliberate collision of my poetry and my journalism.

Tom's Old Boots

        side by side – heavy with
field where he
left them, by the lamb
smell, the cabbage smell,
the boiling potatoes of Mary's open
kitchen door –
she by the stove, fussing and dithering,
scraping the carrots.

Mary's son came from
Canada, as quickly as he could.
It's July, but he notices
she is wearing
        a sweater –
        as if her body, too, is
ground-cold.

She's made too much gravy. She's made
too much everything. It hasn't been a week yet.

Look,   Dad's muddy boots, still
        on guard where he left them,
thinks the son in his chair.
We should have buried them with him –
Tom's boots, shrouded in clay.

I must tidy up,
thinks Mary at the stove.
Those old boots are of no use to anyone.

She knows the weight
of each boot in her hand – how
on the outside,
they speak of the cattle,
and on the inside,
they speak of
Tom's feet.

A wadded up wool sock –
rubbed his toe where she darned it.

                                Boots! says
the toddling granddaughter,
held in the frame of Mary's kitchen door.

She carefully places
a whole leg
in each boot,
her short body swaying
but not
falling.

Laughing
            and laughing,
                        she
                  stands
in the doorway,
in the boots,
in Tom's smoothed leather linings.

DANIELLE **WALKER**

I am a Victoria transplant; I moved here from the Fraser Valley after giving up on hairdressing in favour of the writing program at UVic. I've been here since 2002 and have accumulated a large black cat, a husband, a collection of Irish linens and many poems. The island has been a fruitful place to live, work and raise our first child.

My poetry is written from the working class perspective I lived in Abbotsford. The south-west corner of our province is a crowded one, and I find that unconsciously reflected in my work. I'm always trying to simplify a poem's environment, but clutter creeps in, inevitably, like my parents' divorce after 27 years, or sexual abuse. Like my father's generation from Trail, BC, my poetry from "the big city" is obsessively trying to get someplace else.

Dad is a first generation Italian-Canadian who grew up in Cominco culture. Though I never lived that life I still have strong ties to the trade world, and the mining world. My poetics are mining old stories and trying to make sense of my own life through this imagery. A decade ago Dad built my first car while I watched. In my work I try to take this inherently masculine world and make it relevant to women as well. In university I read Bronwen Wallace and Al Purdy. These are two important voices for me. I learned from them that poetry can, and probably should, act like a group of mechanics or hairdressers on a smoke break telling stories.

Car Incantation

Robert has the credit card
to steal a piecemeal tank
to retreat, repeat the Lougheed
from Mission.

Cars like reel-to-reel
players, carry us back
and forth over the Port Mann
bridge, where wheels squeal,

stop. Play: Robert ruptures
a Kokanee can, his stubble
rubs it like match sticks struck
to light smokes after Cokes
and fries swamped in wallpaper-

paste gravy. The leaves swim in
sunset shearing shadows
in his acne as he tears into me.
I recede under his hands pushing

and pulling. The tank splashes
under my head in the heaving
hatchback. There's nothing
no stars, no moon
in the rear-view drainspout sky.

Cars, like galaxies
leave me cloud-eyed, dropped

on my driveway, mouth still
stained with supreme,
skin scarred the shape
of his hot stone hands.

ANNA **WÄRJE**

Anna Wärje graduated from the Langley Fine Arts High School with a major in Creative Writing, and now studies at the University of British Columbia. Anna's work has recently appeared in *Room Magazine, Event,* and *Dalhousie Review,* and is forthcoming in the anthology *Cleavage,* published by Sumach Press. In January 2008, she was awarded second place in the Vancouver International Writers Festival Poetry Contest, and she was nominated for inclusion in the *2008 Best New Poets Anthology.*

It's not an easy thing, at this stage, for me to write a statement about my poetry. While I have already begun to develop what one calls a "style," the places to which my writing will take me remain largely unknown. For a while in my earlier twenties, my poems tended to bring me back a few years to my small hometown of 100 Mile House and the internal life of a young girl trying to grow in a space that felt too restricted. Now, I am more inclined to go back home and sit amongst the sage bushes and write about the surprising, spreading landscape I couldn't see for my own limbs in the way. For me, poetry is comfortable and necessary. I consider it to be the most perfect form of writing. A poem is simple but not easy. It's concise but incalculable. It may be old but, if good, it is ageless. It's been everywhere. You've never seen it before.

The Present Moment

– On Virginia Woolf

The striking of the hour—
the moment.
It is enough to fill my pockets with stones,
pull my trudging steps through a thicket
of my own words, my waiting,
to where the long land ends in water.

I have no time
to lift blooms that trail their heads in the river,
weave them with my hair
for a lover, a brother to speak oaths upon.
Words, words, words.
Such a waste of them.

No time! To find a boat and
write my name about its prow,
push free toward the towered city,
blind.
And call it a curse! not to see every,
every thing.

Now, therefore, she could write,
and write she did.
She wrote. She wrote. She wrote.

I look at my hands. Can these
be my hands?
They are nothing to me–
illumined starkly
like a moth in the last black second of light
that consumes it.

The present
moment. It is
enough to make a centuries'
wanderer lie down in the

oak shadow and die.

BETSY **WARLAND**

Betsy Warland has published ten books of poetry and prose. Her latest book, *only this blue* (The Mercury Press, 2005), is comprised of a long poem by that name and an essay on poetry. She is the director of The Writer's Studio at Simon Fraser University and is a manuscript consultant for Vancouver Manuscript Intensive (www.betsywarland. com).

The structure of poem is before, after, inside and outside of words. We call it rhythm, rhyme, pattern, meter, cadence, tone. We call it the poem's musicality, form, impulse.

Poem is a wave. At poem's base is the depth of our unknowing. At its crest our knowing. In the movement between – poem's urgent momentum. Because poem's very form acknowledges both what can be said or known, and never said or known, poetry may be as close as we come through language to the sacred. Lyric form is the lineage of poem, as it is of sacred and mystical texts.

Poetry, as music, is intrinsically an airborne art form: poem must navigate page like a voice in space. The body breathes the poem breathes the page. When poem and the poet's body share a profound intimacy, poem and page become lovers – nose to nose – inhaling/exhaling one another's breath. Scored spaces inhale. Scored lines exhale.

Poem's inscribed spaces may mean different things to different people, but these meanings do not need to be specified. The uninscribed space of the page is a powerful form of communication, as is silence: often both are mistaken for emptiness, excess, or as being extrinsic. Poetry is a riptide where language and silence negotiate one another's equally powerful currents.

The integrity of poem hinges on its set of specific circumstances. Just as a composer tends to write choral music to move through a cathedral's time and space, or a lullaby to move through domestic time and space, so the poet composes each poem.

Poetry arouses us via devotion to articulating sensation, uncoiling perception – not by proof or explanation. Poem enters your heart the way idea enters your mind.

Notebook

The net of belief we throw over one another
finding it ever empty
or ensnared
with what we didn't want.

     Baited line of –
beachcomber of –
             belief,
a tear of gratitude
          the only reliable measure.

The buoy of belief –
nothing more perilous than the eyes
that once embraced you.

     Copious kelptongues of belief
shushing any outcry
as you're pulled down
               be leaf
                 belie
beleag.

To be without belief.

               Curious
        as the harbour seal surfacing in front of you –
             a tender memory
            of something vital in its face
– you have
forgotten.

M.C. **WARRIOR**

Born and mostly educated in England, M.C. Warrior worked as a coast logger for seven years and a commercial fisherman (salmon seine and herring gillnet) for nearly twenty-five years. He has also spent a year as an Organiser for the United Fishermen & Allied Workers' Union, a summer writing the official history of Tunnel & Rock Workers' Local 168 of the Laborers' International Union of North America (LIUNA), and four years as a Fisheries Renewal BC partner group's Co-ordinator. He now works as a researcher for LIUNA's Western Canada sub-region.

Si artem requieris, lege.
Which may be translated for these purposes as "If you seek his poetic statement, read." – a crib from the eulogy to Sir Christopher Wren in St Paul's Cathedral.

Metamorphosis

nowadays i yearn even for dreary Tomis:
its desolate winters, fly-blown summers,
and dismal evenings blighted
by torpid local wits
and the club-footed
doggerel of some oaf
of a provincial poetaster.

all of us here beyond the Styx are tormented
by such regrets; but i am doubly damned
by nostalgia not only for that detested city
of my exile, but also for those early days
of my death when the living still praised
my "sweet, witty soul"
and i was the envy of all hell.

no longer.

now the flayed corpse of my verse
is deconstructed and psychoanalysed
for evidence of crimes unknown
even to Octavian. observing me,
pinned and labelled like a museum butterfly,
my fellow wraiths jeer

while i curse the day Erato
seduced me into betraying
my promising career as a barrister
pleading in junior magistrate's court.

TOM **WAYMAN**

Tom Wayman's seventeenth book of poetry is *High Speed Through Shoaling Water* (2007). In 1979 he co-founded the Vancouver Industrial Writers' Union — an important contributor to the work writing movement for nearly 20 years. He was also a key founder in 1984 of the Vancouver Centre of the Kootenay School of Writing, and in 1991 of the writing program at Nelson's Kootenay School of the Arts. He has edited six poetry anthologies, two collections of cultural essays and, in 2007, published collections of short fiction and of novellas. He lives in Winlaw, BC, and teaches at the University of Calgary.

At the core of my poetic practice has been a determination to bring into contemporary literature an accurate, insider's depiction of how our employment affects our lives both on and off the job. Daily work is where we reproduce society every day — not just the goods and services we all depend on, but the power relations that control how a society functions. My writing, and my efforts as an anthologist, have been involved in articulating the social and personal conditions, attitudes and beliefs refashioned anew every day at our jobs. My writing has also focused on the traditional themes of English-language poetry: love, nature, death. Most people, though, experience these facets of life where they can find work. But, especially in BC, some people chose to live where they are surrounded by beauty — and nowhere is this more true than in the Slocan Valley, where I've had a home for 20 years. Still, you can pick up anthology after anthology of any national literature — including Canadian — that presents a literary portrait of a country in which nobody works. You can attend reading after reading at literary festivals and never know that the governing experience of most human beings' lives is the job they have or want. I believe there is an urgent need for work to be the central concern of art, of literature, as it is of human existence.

Yet in the Chilean poet Pablo Neruda's 1971 Nobel Prize lecture, he states that any poet who tries to decree what or how other poets should write, and any poet who tries to defend herself or himself from claims that her or his poems are deficient in some way are equally misled by vanity. I also believe in the truth of Neruda's point.

Snow Right To The Water

I

Under white humps
where the forest
spills down low banks
to the corner of the lawn,
my exhausted parents sleep.
Nothing moves
in the late December day.
The austere cold
means the limbs of the evergreens
surrounding the house
are frosted, while on the ridge
and across fields
alder, birch, aspen bear
atop each branch and twig
thick blossoms of white.

         The only sound
is a distant snowplow grating south along the highway
on the Valley's further side.

         To be dead
is more tiring than the living imagine.
To assert yourself, remain a presence,
haunt through the yellowing Spring,
hot winds of Summer
requires energy the dead
barely possess--even if,
released from hibernation in March,
they are supposed to be rested.
By Autumn, the strain
is evident: memory now
is reflexive, the dead merely
coast amid the weakened sun,
steadily descending leaves.

In Winter

the dead are most dead
--this season of binaries
a manifestation closest to their own
state: white/black, chill/heated.
Even breath, even the passage of
we living across the earth
is rendered visible. The dead, though,
my parents,
lie very still, at one
with the brittle world. Not breathing.
Insensate. Passive
despite blizzard, early dark,
frozen boughs snapped off.

II

On wires overlooking the marsh
near the bridge to the back road
an owl perches in the waning afternoon
to stare across the river

                       that rarely freezes,
that transports its icy fluid
toward an ocean whose shore is covered with snow
to the utmost edge of the tide.

ZACHARIAH **WELLS**

Zachariah Wells, originally from Prince Edward Island, lived in Ottawa, Halifax, Nunavut and Montreal before moving to BC in 2007. He is the author of *Unsettled* (Insomniac Press); the editor of *Jailbreaks: 99 Canadian Sonnets* (Biblioasis); co-author, with wife Rachel Lebowitz, of the children's book *Anything but Hank!* (Biblioasis); and reviews editor for *Canadian Notes & Queries* magazine. His critical essays and reviews have been published widely and he has twice won *Arc* magazine's Critic's Desk Award. Since 2004, he has worked seasonally onboard the train for Via Rail. He can be found online at www.zachariahwells.com.

I suspect that the principal reason I've stuck with writing poems as long as I have is that poetry is sufficiently varied to hold the interest of someone with my gnat's-life attention span. With each new poem I attempt something I've not already done. I've always liked Randall Jarrell's observation that writing poetry is like playing pin the tail on the donkey, only there's no tail and no donkey.

I also appreciate GK Chesterton's bon mot about free verse being, like free love, a contradiction in terms. But I dislike the dogmatic orthodoxies of neo-formalism. I strongly suspect that the herding instinct of such folk — whose insistence on the old is as wrongheaded as the soi-disant avant-garde's rejection of it — is a case of strength in numbers disguising the weakness of individual members and of ideology trumping the harder work of thought. Not that there aren't skilled and intelligent poets to be found within the ranks of these schools and movements, but the all-too-human predilection toward clannishness is antipodal to the achievements of poetry, which are always individual and never predictable.

I tend to favour concrete specifics and the thick consonance of the Anglo-Saxon word hoard — except when an abstraction is necessary and can only be fitly phrased in Latinate diction. I'm impelled to compression, unless the rhetorical posture of a given speaker — all of whom and none of which are identical to me — calls for redundant sprawl. I have an anti-poetic inclination towards the conventionally ugly, but a soft spot for the sublime. I find irony irresistible, especially in a lyrical mood.

I like my poems to speak and sing; I like them to dance and drink, philosophize and philander. I like them to live and I try not to judge their choices too harshly. Usually, I'm less than successful.

Heron, False Creek

There, Heron, you stand
in my shadow, stick pegs
and twigged feet steeped
in the freezing Creek's

shallows, scissor-beaked
slink neck stapled
to a feathered bundle.
There, Heron, you stand,

avatar of angler's
waiting, waiting, calm
as monks praying, steeped
in the shitty Creek's

tide-drained stink—
then tensile—blink—
like a Singer's
stainless needle,

that scissor beak
stabs the reeking
Creek, springs back
with silver, flipping,

flashing in the seawall
lamp standard's
glare. With a slurp
and a shake, like

a puffy glutton
at Monk's Oyster Bar
(stilted in False Creek's
salted shallows)

sucking a shucked mollusk
from its crusted
shell, you swallow,
Heron, stand there

in my shadow, stare
up at the seawall,
skronk, and awkwardly
flop up into the air.

GEORGE **WHIPPLE**

George Whipple was born in Saint John, NB in 1927, graduated from Vancouver Normal School, but spent most of his working life as a Records Clerk for the City of Toronto. He retired in 1985 to Burnaby, BC where he's writing his 13th book of poetry, sketching, translating French poetry and enjoying jazz. His books include; *Tom Thomson and Other Poems* and *The Colour of Memory* from Penumbra Press. *Carousel, Hats Off To The Sun, Fanfares,* and *Kites,* from Ekstasis Press. His work has appeared in 14 anthologies.

Not what I feel but what others feel is my aim in writing. Spontaneity gives life. Technique — enduring form. Poets are born and give up early or spend the rest of their lives perfecting their craft.

Poetry speaks to the most intimate depths of the mind and soul through language worn thin by utilitarian speech. It lacks the purity of the painter's and musician's materials but strives to incorporate those advantages by means of imagery, the harmonious use of vowels, the percussion of consonants and melodious meter, not forgetting thought, which is the line as in a drawing.

No one knows where a poem is going as one writes, nor if it is good or bad, nor what it means. This knowledge comes after the fervour of creation in the dissecting room where the critical faculty (the true measure of genius) must choose, cut, add, rearrange and give the work that inevitability where every letter contributes to the reader's pleasure.

A poem does not exist until it's read. It is a balance between the vernacular and the oracular. Although my poetry enjoys a variety of forms and subject, none of these were premeditated but arrived beneath my hand as I wrote. I like to average one concrete noun per line to keep the poem from sliding off the page, and I like to firm the texture and tighten the syntax by beginning my lines with any word but a conjunction.

Millpond

This painting
  of a millpond
    green and still
Beneath warm summer skies,
  I thought I knew,
    but not now.

I'm almost sure
  that humpbacked heron
    standing on one leg
and staring out at me,
  was not there
    before.

And I wonder
  if I turn my back
    and turn back
again, if that intruder
  will have unfurled
    its great grey wings
    and be gone

from that painted world,
  continuing its journey
    to a place beyond
      the gilded frame,
as in my tarnished frame,
  I too am only
    a sojourner.

RITA **WONG**

The author of *monkeypuzzle* (Press Gang, 1998) and *forage* (Nightwood, 2007), Rita Wong received the Asian Canadian Writers Workshop Emerging Writer Award in 1997 and the Dorothy Livesay Poetry Prize in 2008. A book-length collaborative poem, *sybil unrest*, co-written with Larissa Lai, is forthcoming with Line Books. She teaches in Critical + Cultural Studies at the Emily Carr University of Art + Design in Vancouver.

poetics begins with my body — a walking, breathing, dreaming bag of water — holding an instrument, out of which another fluid, ink, releases. this body whose tributaries learn and benefit from the poems of shirley bear, jeannette armstrong, lee maracle, chrystos, marie annharte baker, kateri akiwenzie-damm, marilyn dumont, connie fife, joanne arnott, janet marie rogers, sharron proulx-turner, joy harjo, and more. how do i pay my respects to this land but by starting with the poems that survive and defy colonization, the poems that move through the air into my eyes, ears, throat, & pulse? acknowledging the work of indigenous women poets anchors an ethical poetics, an imagining of a possible future that spirals backward and forward from filaments of collective memory. a place to start: respecting the voices that arise from native land so courageously, and dare i say, generously. a generosity that inspires, breathes-life-into, reciprocity and redress. having inherited a history of violence, attempted genocide, displacement and land theft, i breathe and walk and write because another world is still somehow possible, one of respectful relations and peaceful coexistence. forage refers not only to my coping mechanism as someone who lives amidst capitalist contradictions — what am i doing in the library, on the internet, at protests, in the farmer's markets and the community food co-ops for that matter, if not foraging for ways to survive and understand crisis — but also a poetics, writing my way through and in the mess. as lee maracle reminds me, i have a responsibility to search out the meaning of colonial robbery and figure out how to undo it. how might perception change if one tries to learn indigenous languages and cultures? a small experiment: in "return" the Halq'eméylem, Ktunaxa, Gitsenimx, Nisgaa, Kwakwala, and Secwepemc words that fracture english come from http://www.firstvoices.com.

return

the city paved over with ~~cement~~ *english cracks open, stubborn* Halq'eméylem *springs up*

among the newspaper boxes and mail receptacles in the shade of the thqa:t

along the sidewalks lined with grass and pta:kwem *waiting to grow anywhere they can*

around the supermarkets full of transported food – kwukemels, *tomatoes, chocolate and chicken.*

under the wet green shelter of chestnut and p'xwelhp *leaves*

carried on the tricky wings of skwówéls, *also known as* qukin, gaak, gwawis, setsé7 *and more in the languages of this land*

more to tree & bracken & cucumber & oak & raven than meets the stiff I
root & stomach & seed speak glottal, gut & gift

DERK **WYNAND**

Derk Wynand has published ten collections of poetry, one of fiction, and five of poetry and fiction translated from the German of H.C. Artmann, Erich Wolfgang Skwara, and Dorothea Grünzweig. *Glass Voices lasinäänet*, his translation of Grünzweig's third poetry collection, is scheduled for fall publication by Buschek Books. A former editor of *The Malahat Review* and twice Chair of the University of Victoria's Department of Writing, he retired into his work in 2004.

In my first post-teenage-blinded-by-love poems, I was a word-skinner, and I still pare words, if less ferociously. I no longer condemn certain parts of speech, like the adjective, as unpoetic, and don't always or consciously use an amputated language. Still, the Imagist lessons stick. While much of the practice of poetry fits Pound's formula, "Dichten = condensare," reducing the fleeting moments to their essentials, some of the process seems about fluffing them up to make them light and also last longer. One approach takes the poetic materials the way we used to take slices of that awful Wonderbread and squeeze them into hard little balls to suck on; the other adds ingredients and turns them into angel cake. One doodles toward haiku, the other twitters toward Rococo. There's plenty of room between and I try to stretch into it.

For nearly two decades now, travel has nudged me toward poems, and specifically travel south: Portugal, Mexico, Cuba. I think it's the way travel forces you to shed routines and see things fresh. When the Douglas fir has become overly familiar, the lemon tree or palm can lead you back to the archetypal tree. In the south, things flourish and decay quickly. The sunset's over too soon, just as you're beginning to enjoy your regrets about mortality. All that high-speed flux feeds the inner restlessness that sometimes leads to poetry: the reaction simultaneously to so much beauty, so much perishability. In Portugal, it's *saudade*, what drives Fado, those songs that make you ache for the very place in which you already are. *Tristesse tropique* might be another label for the process, and even *Weltschmerz*, though the latter term would have to be adjusted a little, so that it's not the cruel weight of the world that pains, but its lightweight, evanescent beauty. The poems I try to find are the ones that make you want to pick at that wound.

Homesick

God, how the dusty fronds of the palms
comb the tangled light.

The way a cormorant dries his wings on shore
and does not fear your approach.
How gracefully the trio of egrets
treads the wet grass beneath your window
and falls from grace when the prey is sighted.

You could listen all night to the saxophonist
squeezing the last notes out of his instrument
and the piano player chasing after him,
or the cicadas when the stars....

How good it would be if your Spanish
went beyond the *huevos fritos* and *pescados*
and *cervezas*, everything you stuff into your mouth,
if you could understand the complex answers
to your simple construct, *¿Que pasa cuando*
Fidel *es muerte*, but.

The wistful looks, but.

The wistful looks of certain women in paintings
at the gallery, keeping their eyes fixed on you
as you step from one to the other.

The more ambiguous look of the beauty
who takes your bag with the digital camera
and its long memory.

The long memory.

How the shells break to reveal their secrets
when the water is too rough for swimming and so,
almost console.

The sheer scale of the monument to José Marti
and its historical shadow over the rubble
in which the poor somehow manage.

How they manage to sing.

What a difference between the smiles
on the Europeans' faces and those
on the Afro-Cubans'.

A Canadian take on
the American take on
the Afro-Cuban take on
the embargo.

How generous a tour the taxi driver gives you.

The image of Che on extra-large Tee-shirts
and on infants' Tee-shirts and on photos
hung in a restaurant where it seems
only the famous have wined and dined.

The fifteen minutes of Fidel's warm gaze
at his loyal following and the lost look
in the eyes of the sick lined up
at the pharmacies.

How all that you've wanted to escape
reconstitutes itself inside the space between
and summons you back.

ONJANA **YAWNGHWE**

Onjana Yawnghwe grew up in Thailand and Vancouver. She has a MA in English, and is the founding editor of Xerography, a little literary journal. Onjana lives in Burnaby with her husband, Shane, and Pique the cat.

My poetry comes from my family's complicated past, which at various times I have met with ignorance, embarrassment, gratefulness and ambivalence. We come from an ethic minority group in Burma (also known as Myanmar), called the Shan, and because of the political violence and tumult in the last 40 years in that country, our family's story is one of escape to Thailand (where I was born), and eventual immigration to Canada. Like many immigrants before and since, the act of transplanting one's life for one that is completely foreign was a immense act of creation. My poems reflect this exhausting effort of self-making in a new land: finding oneself relieved and hopeful, finding oneself trying to understand a new language and way of life, trying not to lose your first language and culture, but inevitably losing bits of your past, finding yourself as a person of the in-between. In some of my poems, there is a lyric undercurrent, but in other poems the language is fragmented, grammar loose, rhythms ragged; the language feels at times unsettled, as I have, at times, felt unsettled. Above all, I write with the realization that no matter how difficult it may have been for me, immigrating to Vancouver was infinitely more difficult for my parents. I write with the knowledge of their sacrifice, I write with a thankfulness for this land, and I write with a heart full of this language which was unknown to me until my 7th year of life.

english lesson

this language gives me life
                                        (what have you done

and swallows me up

                                        (with the tongue of curves and curlicues

    an insect in a in a fish on a hook in a fire
    like a gem in a stone in a fist opening

                                        (want want to shut their mouths with bleeding fists

--

hey where'dya get your clothes
           hummed air of laundromats

why does your apartment smell
           immigrant shoes tied-up-to-the-neck shirts

face it you're just nothin' but a refugee   *(onelanguage subtracts another*
           scuffed jeans from one side of mouth

whatsa matter cantcha speak english

                                        (what happened to the face you used to wear

--

running after me a wild shan girl yelling
kicking earth her ignorant knees
can't write but laughs freely and mocks in
tongue loose lips wide as my hips in scorn

when I learn my silence she stops   *want*
giggles disappear
knit mouth to tongue   *want*
ragged breath in my ear

                                                     you never get

--

do you listen to the rain and imagine it speaking to you?
do you believe crows call out to you in early morning?

it's a sin to lose the language of your birth
first words so tenderly sung by your cheek
a dying pant in the ear:
who are you now but an invasion?

PATRICIA **YOUNG**

Patricia Young has published one collection of short fiction and nine collections of poetry, most recently, *Here Come the Moonbathers* (Biblioasis, 2008). She has won the Dorothy Livesay Award, the Pat Lowther Award and has twice been nominated for the Governor General's Award for poetry. In 2007/08 she was the writer-in-residence at the University of New Brunswick.

What I love about a poem is the mystery of it, the line that arrives out of nowhere, that defies meaning, transcends it, the image that does and does not make sense, that explodes in the nether regions of the brain. Words that transport. Turn us on our heads. The poem that gives meaning to experience, expands and shapes it, returns us to ourselves, speaks to our collective spirit, that place within each of us that seems always to be incomplete.

I think of the student who rarely spoke in workshops and when she did she spoke softly, in brief, rapid-fire sentences. Once, walking out of the room at the end of class, she said, almost inaudibly, as though this fact had just occurred to her, "I write poems because I can't speak."

"Yes," I said. "I do too."

I was in my forties, had been writing poetry for most of my adult life, but it was the first time I realized this was true.

I think of my friend who says all she wants is to write one true thing. I love the humility of those words, the modest desire and ambition, the poet in her who will struggle to do just that.

Boys

Day-glo idiots, hapless visionaries.
Boys were boys, we weren't particular.
Words bunched in their fists but what did we care?
We wanted the lazy and fuzzy-cheeked,
the ones who went ape-shit over girls

who blew smoke in their faces and came
with six month warranties. Boys
who made careers out of playing the freak.
Winsome, awkward, brilliant. Why not?
Zen-boys with buttery apricot skin,

legs slung over our legs, purring like huge cats.
The fast talkers in sepia tones, the algebra
boys untangling the tangoed equation
at the heart of Latina girls. Our logic
was circular. We wanted them

because we wanted them.
Though it wore us down, reduced us
to tears. And still we wanted to go
where they went, to not be afraid
of what they wanted. Who wanted them?

We did, us, the hippy chicks and ice queens,
the brainiacs and girls so ordinary
there was nothing to distinguish us
except the depth of our wanting.
The mind balks at how much, how far back.

Let me explain exactly what we had in mind:
the quixotic and hardcore guitar-pluckers,
the sci-fi nerds beaming radioactive
light into our rec rooms. We wanted them
and didn't want them, but mostly

we wanted boys, loaded as questions,
simple as widgets. The sensitive Lotharios
in blazing white gym gear,
the ones who kept shooting themselves
in the foot, the mouth, into orbit.

We tried to want other things, fashion magazines,
tennis lessons, class C drugs, but nothing
came close to a sweetly vagrant boy
inside a Goodwill drop-off box. Whose
fault was it? That our kneecaps wanted them,

our mandibles, cartilage, tendons, ligaments,
you name it, every bit of us wanted them, despite
their roving eyes, their fumbling monkey love.
The more we wanted boys the more
we wanted boys. How dumb was that?

To want the gritty sex scene in them,
the tryst, the future affair. Boys who wanted
us as much as we wanted them. Or did they?
We didn't ask. Didn't dare. Wanted them starkers,
artfully thrown, like clay against the wall.

More than the Catholic girls wanted them,
girls who scrapped behind the cathedral
over boys other boys wanted. Wanted them
despite our mothers' warnings, those bare-faced
liars who refused to admit they'd also wanted

boys who'd brought them to the reservoir,
and then to their knees. Not knowing
it would take the rest of our lives to get over them –
what they said to us, what they did
with their tongues. We were obsessive,

insufferable, chained ourselves to them
the way eco warriors chain themselves
to bulldozers and trees. What choice did we have
but to trap them the way we'd once trapped
frogs, ducklings, other forms of innocent

swamp life. They played us for suckers and fools
and still we went back, wanting. Boys. Just boys.
God help us, we were doomed before we began,
hardwired to want even the loudmouth
punks letting off firecrackers at dawn.

DAVID **ZIEROTH**

David Zieroth's most recent book of poetry is *The Village of Sliding Time* (Harbour, 2006). He lives in North Vancouver, BC. He has also published *Crows Do Not Have Retirement* (Harbour, 2001), poems, and a memoir, *The Education of Mr. Whippoorwill: A Country Boyhood* (Macfarlane Walter and Ross, 2002). He won the Dorothy Livesay Poetry Prize for *How I Joined Humanity at Last* (Harbour, 1998).

Recently I've been telling my friends there are two kinds of poets, ecstatic and articulate (not just the old romantic/classical dichotomy, or not quite). The ecstatic can't write unless he's moved by intimations seemingly arriving from elsewhere and overwhelming him into speech, whereas the articulate follows an inkling and digs around and burrows past his present knowledge to find what must be revealed.

I say I'm of the articulate type and most of my poet-friends are ecstatic, though a few say I'm really the ecstatic and afraid, according to this analysis, of giving up control, of relying on the visitation of the divine muse rather than on the exploratory inner workings of the human spirit. Perhaps they imagine I can access a world-soul and remain unafraid of its daemon beat and its rush of connective, instinctive foresight.

Such thoughts never occur to me when I'm writing — then it's all ferreting and digging and ransacking for word and tone and line, and rhythm, and waiting, and not thinking, but letting what's missing and needed take its path to me. Averting my eyes in order to see more clearly aslant, as has famously been said. Pretending to drift (and actually drifting) to complete necessary sifting. Following the golden inkling-thread and finding delectable ambiguity. Failing to find, petering out, stalling in portending-to-lukewarm non-ness.

So mutually ecstatic and articulate? Perhaps twain modes — intertwining and fructifying and amassing and delivering and then going silent, soporifically silent, while really gathering for the next poem, which can never — to me — be imagined before it arrives from spaces out or in or both.

Sinking

One morning he woke up and started sinking
down through flannel sheets, through foam
through each airspace in foam, his fingers
clutching what he kept missing, missing it
when he opened his hand, nothing there and
the same nothing kept with him as he sank

down through cloth, coils and then
through his parquet floor, and he panicked
when he entered the ceiling of those
who lived below—but they were workers
and they had already left, their bed sheets
untidy, and he couldn't help noting

pants on the floor, a tube of lipstick tipped
on the dresser, its lid off, the living colour
alarmingly red, and he descended
through shag rug musty with crumbs
and unswept hairs, sock fuzz, toenails
and once a glitzy button passed by

He began to relax now he knew he could
manage ceilings and floors, believing
he would stop when he met hard earth
so down through six discrete floors
he fell, slowly, almost as one drifting, not
plummeting, not a disaster, just a descent

He waved goodbye to operational apparatus
in the basement and then easily entered
concrete and felt the first brisk cold muscle
of buried earth so long removed from light
and incalescence, and knew he would continue
until he met the central fire of the globe

and he wondered if heat at the heart
would be his final immolating destination
if that forge would provide the brake
he needed—but already he was thinking
it hardly mattered where he finally ceased
because the journey toward heat would be

long, long, much longer than six floors
and he would need to settle into accepting
this fate if he wanted any clear mind left
when he came face to face with molten flame
calling him, undoubtedly calling, though last night
he could not have imagined any such sound

ACKNOWLEDGEMENTS

Permission has hereby been granted to Donna Kane to use four lines from Al Purdy's "Idiot's Song" from *Beyond Remembering* (Harbour Publishing 2000).

One line from "Shiva" by Robinson Jeffers, in Russell Thornton's poem "Nest of Swan's Bones," from Jeffers, Robinson, *The Collected Poetry of Robinson Jeffers*, edited by Tim Hunt, Volume 2, 1928-1938, copyright 1938, renewed 1966 by Donnan Jeffers and Garth Jeffers; copyright The Jeffers Literary Properties. Used with the permission of Stanford University Press.

Quote from K. Simms, *Paul Ricoeur*, London, New York: Routledge (2003), used with thanks in Daniela Elza's poem "true or false (a triptych."

Thanks to Peter Haase, Sophia Haase, Paris Haase, Diane Rhenisch, Phyllis Webb, Gary Geddes, Jean Mallinson, Robert Reid, Ursula Vaira and Tom Wayman for advice and support, Murray Reiss for copy-editing assistance, and Diana Dean for use of her painting.

SOURCES:

1954- *British Columbia a Centennial Anthology*, ed. Reginald Eyre Watters, M&S.

1974- *Woman's Eye: 12 BC poets*, ed. Dorothy Livesay, AIR Press.

1975- *A Government Job At Last: an anthology of working poems, mainly Canadian*, ed. Tom Wayman, MacLeod's Books.

1975- *Pomegranate: A Selection of Vancouver Poetry*, ed. Nellie McClung, Intermedia Press.

1975- *Skookum Wawa: Writings of the Canadian Northwest*, ed. Gary Geddes, Oxford.

1977- *Western Windows: A Comparative Anthology of Poetry of British Columbia*, ed. Patricia M. Ellis, CommCept Publishing.

1977- *New: West Coast: 72 contemporary british columbia poets*, ed. Fred Candelaria, Intermedia Press.

1979- *D'Sonoqua: An Anthology of Women Poets of British Columbia, Vol I & II*, ed. Ingrid Klassen, Intermedia Press.

1985- *Shop Talk*, ed. Tom Wayman, Pulp Press.

1986- *Vancouver*, Soul of A City, ed. Gary Geddes, D&Mc.

1986- *Vancouver Poetry*, ed. Allan Safarik, Polestar Press.

1989- *A Labour of Love*, an anthology of poetry on pregnancy and childbirth, ed. Mona Fertig, Polestar Press.